UNFORGETTABLE NY ISLANDERS

GAMES & MOMENTS FROM THE PRESS BOX, ICE & FRONT OFFICE

BY: MATTHEW BLITTNER

ISBN: 978-0-578-64707-4
ISBN-13: 978-0-578-64707-4

DEDICATION

In this world, it's not enough to merely believe in yourself. Rather, you need others to believe in you as well.

To that end, this book would not have been completed without the support of my family and friends.

Specifically, I'd like to dedicate this book to my parents -- Mandi and Seth -- and sister Tara for their constant support even during the toughest times. And to my friends -- Arianna Rappy, Stef Hicks, Leanna Gryak, Maggie Wince, Walt Bonné, Daniel Greene, Jared Fertig, Jason Russo, Peter Koutros and Robert DeVita -- who were always there for me when I needed them and I thank them for that.

CONTENTS

INTRODUCTION

"LET'S GO ISLANDERS!"

For nearly 50 years fans of the New York Islanders have uttered this phrase as a rallying cry, trying desperately to will their team to victory. And more often than not, they have succeeded.

As the 2019-2020 season (the 47th season in franchise history) marches onward, the Islanders find themselves trying to once again capture Lord Stanley's fabled chalice -- The Stanley Cup. And while that is the goal of every NHL franchise, some have more success than others at seeing the journey through to the end.

Since their inception in the fall of 1972, the Isles have won The Cup a staggering FOUR TIMES, with all four coming in consecutive years from 1980-83. Not bad for a franchise that was hastily granted life by the National Hockey League as part of a plan to keep the WHA (World Hockey Association) out of Long Island.

Before you exclaim, "WHAT?!" please let me explain.

From 1942 to 1966, the NHL operated as a six-team league, known as the Original Six Era. During those 25-years, the Boston Bruins, Chicago Blackhawks, Detroit Red Wings, Montreal Canadiens, New York Rangers and Toronto Maple Leafs battled each other for NHL supremacy.

But in 1967 the league decided to add six more teams to the mix; thus kick starting The Expansion Era. And for awhile, new franchises were added every couple of years.

Then, in November of 1971, the NHL granted a franchise to Roy Boe, who also owned the New York Nets (then of the ABA and now in the NBA). But this wasn't a cut and dried expansion plan, for you see, the WHA (World Hockey Association) was interested in placing a team of its own in the confines of Long Island's Nassau Veterans Memorial Coliseum.

However, local politicians didn't want the WHA coming to town and in an effort to prevent such a thing from happening, brought in renowned lawyer, William Shea for help. After all, who better to handle this situation than the man who helped bring the New York Mets into existence a decade earlier.

With Shea's assistance, NHL President Clarence Campbell was brought into the mix and plans for an NHL franchise to come to Long Island began to take shape. There was just one problem -- the New York Rangers.

According to the NHL's geographic outline, Long Island was technically Rangers territory and the Original Six franchise wanted no part of having to compete with another NHL team in the area. But after some thought, Blueshirts' President, Bill Jennings decided to allow the Long Island based NHL franchise; for a fee of course.

On November 8, 1971, the Long Island franchise was officially granted to Boe for the sum total of $11 million ($5 million of which was paid to the Rangers as a territorial fee).

With the founding of the soon-to-be-named Islanders, the WHA gave up on its plan to put a franchise in the newly built Nassau Coliseum and the NHL had gained a 15th team. The Atlanta Flames were then added as the 16th team to prevent an unbalanced schedule.

The Islanders had life, but no roster or structure as the calendar flipped from 1971 to 1972, but that changed in February of '72 as Bill Torrey was named the team's inaugural General Manager; a title he would hold until the summer of 1992.

Torrey wasn't exactly put in a situation to succeed early on, as the NHL's expansion draft rules were nothing like they are today. Whereas in 2017, the Vegas Golden Knights benefitted from new rules that allowed an expansion franchise to succeed right away, the Islanders had no such help back in 1972.

Luckily, Torrey was smart, he knew that by accepting underwhelming players from the other teams' rosters, he would eventually be able to use that to his advantage and truly build his team by means of the NHL's annual entry draft.

However, that's not to say the Isles didn't get at least a few key players, as they were able to acquire Ed Westfall, Gerry Hart and Billy Smith in the Expansion Draft. Specifically, Westfall became the franchise's first captain and Smith was a rock in net for well over a decade.

Not only did Torrey luck out with the trio of Westfall, Hart and Smith, but he also began to build out his roster when he selected Billy Harris, Lorne Henning and Bobby Nystrom in the Amateur Draft. All that was left was to find a Head Coach and that gig eventually went to Phil Goyette.

With their roster set and most of the management positions filled, the Isles headed into their first season looking to make a name for themselves.

Alas, they started the year with 13 losses in their first 17 games, including an Opening Night loss to their expansion brother, the Atlanta Flames. And while they did rebound to win their next game -- a 3-2 victory over the Los Angeles Kings five nights later -- it was a moment that was ultimately overshadowed by the team's underwhelming record. Rather than being a springboard of hope, the Islanders quickly established that this was simply not their year; finishing with a record of 12-60-6. That futility even led to Goyette's ouster after 48 games, as he was replaced behind the bench by Earl Ingarfield.

Unfortunately, Ingarfield did no better than Goyette and after the season he was let go in favor of Al Arbour; a man who would eventually become synonymous with the Islanders.

But first came the 1973-74 season and while a record of 19-41-18 doesn't seem like much on the surface, it did represent a 26-point increase for the team; which proved to be a portent of things to come as that would be the last season in which the Islanders failed to qualify for the playoffs until the 1988-89 campaign a whopping 15-years later.

And besides, thanks to the Isles on-ice misfortune in their first two seasons, they were able to draft players such as: Denis Potvin, Clark Gillies and Bryan Trottier; each of whom would play an important role for the team in the years to come.

Now that Torrey's plan to build the team organically was in motion, the next step was to see an improvement in the team's record. And boy did they improve.

The 1974-75 season gave birth to a number of firsts for the young Islanders franchise. They finished above .500 for the first time and they also advanced to the playoffs for the first time, courtesy of a 32-point increase in the standings from the season prior.

Granted, they still "only" tallied 88-points, so it's not like much was expected of them when the playoffs began. But boy were those people wrong!

The Isles first-ever playoff opponent was their geographic rival, the New York Rangers. How apropos that the team that initially didn't even want the Islanders to exist was now going to be their first playoff challenger. Of course, nobody expected the Isles to do much against the battle-tested Rangers; even if it was a short best-two-of-three series.

So, naturally, the Isles won Game 1 -- at Madison Square Garden no less -- by the score of 3-2 and were now just one win away from knocking off the favored Rangers.

But not so fast, for the Rangers came back and won Game 2 at Nassau Coliseum 8-3; thus setting the stage for a winner-take-all Game 3 back at MSG.

It was a close game and one that many expected the Rangers to eventually pull out. But the Isles forced overtime and just 11 seconds into the extra period J.P. Parise scored the overtime, series-clinching goal to stun the Madison Square Garden crowd and send the Islanders into the second-round, where they would face the Pittsburgh Penguins.

It was an unforgettable moment for sure, but one the Islanders would soon top in death-defying fashion.

The Islanders had to be feeling good about themselves as the series against Pittsburgh started, but that good feeling quickly turned to dread for many as the Isles fell down 0-3 in the series and were in danger of being swept out of the playoffs in front of their hometown fans.

Was this where the Islanders' magic would end? I mean, not even the most die-hard of Isles fans could have expected the team to make it this far? Their presumed second-round exit was still progress compared to the previous two seasons.

NOT. SO. FAST.

As the Islanders hosted Game 4 at Nassau Coliseum the players, as well as the coaching staff and management, all adopted a policy of taking things one shift at a time. Nothing more. Nothing less.

And that philosophy worked, as the hometown team staved off elimination with a 3-1 victory; at least for one night.

As the teams reconvened in Pittsburgh for Game 5, it quickly became apparent that the Islanders were no one-trick pony, for the team again received a stay of execution via a 4-2 victory in front of the hostile Pittsburgh crowd.

Now things were beginning to get interesting. Not since the 1941-42 Maple Leafs had an NHL team comeback from being down 0-3 in a best-four-of-seven playoff series to win the series. Granted, the Isles still had to win Game 6 at home and then go back to Pittsburgh for a potential Game 7 before they could etch their names alongside those of the Leafs, but something felt different for the team. And that something was about to rewrite the record books.

In front of their home crowd the Islanders again denied Pittsburgh's wish of winning the series; this time handing the Penguins a 4-1 loss and setting the stage for a winner-take-all Game 7 back in Pittsburgh two nights later.

For the Penguins, the premise of a Game 7 at home had to be equal parts exhilarating and frightening. On the one hand, they were coming home and clearly felt they would have the proverbial "hometown advantage." But they also had to be worried about fixing what was ailing them; namely the fact that their once burgeoning offense had gone into an early slumber.

On the other side of things, the Isles were relaxed as could be; knowing they were playing with house money, even if nobody wanted to admit it.

Game 7 was as tightly contested of an affair as you could get, as both teams remained scoreless into the third period. But that soon changed as Isles captain, Ed Westfall scored late in the period for the only goal of the game, propelling the Islanders to the series-clinching win and writing their names in the history books as the second team in NHL history to comeback from being down 0-3 in the series to comeback and win it in seven.

For the Penguins, it was a nightmare they could not wake up from. For the Isles, it was sheer elation. But their miracle run wasn't over yet, as the Flyers were waiting for them in Philadelphia. And just like against Pittsburgh, the Islanders fell down 0-3 in the series to the Flyers. It had taken a miracle for the Isles to comeback against the Penguins. Surely they couldn't make another? Or could they?

Calling on their experiences from the previous round the Islanders again stormed back from being down 0-3 to tie the series and force a winner-take-all Game 7!

What was going on? Just who were these Islanders?! What magical power allowed them to routinely stave off elimination and be victorious?

Well, perhaps it wasn't actually magic, but rather heart that allowed them to make the impossible seem so possible. But before the Islanders could complete their second miracle comeback, they finally fell victim to the Flyers in Game 7, by the score of 4-1, down in Philadelphia; thus ending their first playoff journey. But not their last.

Inspired by the events of their 1975 playoff campaign, the Isles looked to finally climb to the top of the mountain in 1976; their eyes collectively fixed on the Stanley Cup. And during the regular season it looked like they might be on their way to achieving their dreams, as they tallied a franchise-best 101-points. Sadly, it was not to be as they ran into the 127-point juggernaut known as the Montreal Canadiens in the Conference Final and were eliminated in five-games.

With the taste of both success and failure lingering in their mouths, the Isles came back in 1977, determined to complete their mission. This time, they tallied 106-points and marched to the Conference Final, where once again, the Canadiens were waiting for them. And this was no ordinary Canadiens team. This was a team that had just set the single-season NHL record for most points with 132!

The Islanders once again fell short against Montreal, but not before pushing the eventual Cup champions to a sixth game; one more than the year prior.

For all their talent and perseverance, the Isles just could not get over that final hump; the one in which, at the end of the day, they hoped would end with them being crowned champions. And to make matters worse, the 1978 season saw them take a step back; even though they finished the regular-season with 111-points, the Islanders fell prey to the underdog Maple Leafs in a seven-game opening round upset.

Things needed to change in 1979 and many thought that this would finally be the Isles year. They tallied an astounding 116-points; the most in the league. And they were heavily favored to go all the way. But once again something was missing.

After sweeping the Chicago Black Hawks in the opening round of the playoffs, the Isles ran into the rival Rangers and were shockingly upset in six-games; the last of which was a 2-1 loss in front of The Coliseum fans.

With back-to-back playoff upsets on their record, many began to fear that the Islanders would never be able to win the big one. The term chokers was even thrown around.

Lucky for the players, coaches and management, nobody inside the organization believed that to be the case. And with Torrey and Arbour leading the way you just knew that they were going to eventually figure things out.

Before the 1979-80 campaign got underway a few changes occurred. For one, Ed Westfall, who had relinquished the captaincy to Clark Gillies the season prior, retired and eventually became one of the team's broadcasters.

Another change came in the form of a new owner. Roy Boe had been the Isles owner since the beginning, but he was losing money and needed out. So he sold the team to John Pickett, who had been a limited partner for several years. And there was one more change as Torrey was given the title of Team President after he helped broker the deal between Boe and Pickett.

As the 1979-80 season got underway, Coach Arbour took a different approach with his team. Rather than forcing them to acquire every last possible point, he began to understand the need for balance. If he could lose a couple battles and still win the war then he'd be sitting pretty. And that's exactly what he did as he led the Isles to "only" 91-points, which were still plenty enough to qualify for the playoffs.

Torrey too saw the need for balance and shortly before the playoffs, he dealt fan-favorite, Billy Harris and veteran defenseman, Dave Lewis to the Los Angeles Kings in exchange for center Butch Goring.

Goring immediately gave the Isles a boost as he solidified the second-line center role that the team so desperately needed to create more balance within its lineup.

And the results were instantaneous.

While marching through the playoffs, the Islanders displayed their newfound abilities as well as their battle-tested wills by winning four overtime games in the first three rounds; the last of which was a double-overtime thriller against the Buffalo Sabres in the second game of their third-round series. That win was delivered by Bobby Nystrom and foreshadowed things to come.

On it was to the Stanley Cup Final, where the Islanders faced off with the regular season champion Flyers. But the Isles were neither scared nor intimidated by the Bruising Flyers. And just to prove that point, they went out and beat the Flyers in Game 1, courtesy of another overtime win; this one delivered by all-world defenseman, Denis Potvin, who scored on the power-play to give New York a 1-0 series lead.

From there the Islanders and Flyers proceeded to split the next four games -- two apiece -- and the series headed to Game 6 at Nassau Coliseum with the Isles prepared for what was -- at that time -- the biggest game in team history.

While the Flyers drew first blood on a power-play goal by Reggie Leach, the Isles responded with two quick goals of their own, one each by Potvin -- on the power-play -- and Duane Sutter, before Philly knotted things at two on a goal by Brian Propp. And that was just the first period!

The second period was all Islanders as Mike Bossy -- on the power-play -- and Bobby Nystrom each scored to give the home team a two-goal lead going into the third period. And of course, they also gave the hometown fans something to cheer about, as everybody in attendance knew the Islanders were just 20 minutes away from the first Stanley Cup championship in franchise history.

But first, hold the celebration, as the Flyers preyed on the Isles old weakness of being unable to close out games when they mattered most and scored two goals, one each from Bob Dailey and John Paddock, to force overtime and have the Islanders and their fans fearing the worst.

Years later, many of the Islanders players admitted that they did not want to have to go back to Philadelphia for a potential Game 7. And many of the writers covering the team echoed that sentiment, fearing that a Game 7 in Philly would surely result in the Isles demise.

Not to worry though, as Nystrom and John Tonelli pulled off a play that they had practiced thousands of times -- but never properly executed -- by crisscrossing just in time to confuse the opposition's defenders. And then all that was left to do was for Nystrom to put the puck past Flyers goalie, Pete Peeters for the overtime-winning, Stanley Cup-clinching goal; thus setting off a raucous celebration that carried on all the way into the wee hours of the next morning and involved everyone from the players to the coaches, to the management to even the broadcasters and writers. And, of course, the fans too!

Their Stanley Cup championship was well deserved, but it was only the beginning, as the Isles went on to win The Cup in each of the following three seasons, for a total of four straight championships.

In 1981 they beat the Minnesota North Stars in five-games. In 1982 they swept the Vancouver Canucks. And in 1983 they swept the high-flying Edmonton Oilers. Four consecutive Cups, it was a feat unmatched by any team other than the Montreal Canadiens, who won five-straight Cups from 1956-1960 and four-straight from 1976-1979.

And with four Cups already in hand, the Isles set out to match Montreal's mark of five-straight; something they hoped to accomplish in 1984.

The Islanders' "Drive For Five" took on a life of its own as the team finished the regular season with 104-points and looked poised to become the second team ever to win five-straight Cups.

A rocky series against the Rangers put the "Drive For Five" in jeopardy early, but the Isles pulled off one of their trademark comebacks to win Games 4 and 5 and down the Blueshirts in the opening round. Up next were the Washington Capitals. And although the Islanders lost Game 1, they won the next four in a row to keep the dream alive.

Then came the Canadiens, who actually won the first two games of the series in an act of defiance, as if to say that they didn't want the Isles to match their record. But New York won the next four in a row to reach the Stanley Cup Final. And more impressively, the win over Montreal gave them an NHL-record 19-consecutive series victories; an absolutely mind-boggling number that has never been close to being matched.

Could the Islanders really win five-straight Cups? The only team left in their way was the Oilers. But these Oilers were different. They weren't the inexperienced high-flyers from the year before. Yes, they were still high-flying, but they were also smarter and that made them an extremely dangerous team.

The teams split the first two games at Nassau Coliseum and many felt the Islanders might just be able to pull another rabbit out of their hat. But that wasn't the case as the series shifted to Edmonton, where the Oilers won three-straight games to end the Isles "Drive For Five."

While the dynasty was over, the Isles were still a formidable team and one that was still a playoff threat. Sadly, no more Cups followed, although, they did have a rather unforgettable encounter with the Capitals during The Spring of 1987.

New York opened the playoffs by losing three of the first four games to the Capitals and looked like their time in the playoffs was nigh. But two straight wins evened the series at three-games apiece and set the stage for a historic Game 7 down in Washington D.C.

The game was played on April 18, 1987, and it was one that nobody who was in attendance that night will ever forget.

Washington's Mike Gartner scored late in the first period to give the Caps a 1-0 lead as the teams headed into the first intermission. But midway through the second period, Pat Flatley scored for the Isles to knot the score at 1-1 before Grant Martin took back the lead for the Caps, who held onto the 2-1 lead as the teams entered the third period.

A Bryan Trottier goal shortly after the midway point of the third period tied the game at 2-2 and that's where the score stayed as the game headed to overtime.

But soon one overtime became two and two eventually became three. Triple overtime games are rare, though not exactly unheard of. But for the reporters covering the game, it was madness as their deadlines were now essentially missed. And down on the ice, the players were on both teams were on the verge of collapsing out of exhaustion.

An end was needed, but three overtime periods weren't enough, so on came a fourth. With all deadlines now officially missed and the players and coaches completely drained, this game teased a complete rewrite of the NHL's record books.

Luckily for all involved, well, maybe not for the Caps, the Isles' Pat LaFontaine scored the game-winning, series-clinching goal at the 8:47 mark of the fourth overtime period to send the Islanders to the next round where the Flyers were waiting for them.

When the game ended it was officially Easter Morning and depending on whose watch you go by, it was either 1:56am or 1:58am when LaFontaine's goal went past goalie Bob Mason. And not to be lost in the shuffle, but Isles goalie Kelly Hrudey also made history by stopping 73 of a possible 75 shots sent his way.

The Isles were tired, yet happy. But they needed to make a quick decision on what to do next, because their series against the Flyers was starting in less than 48 hours.

Should they go home, get some sleep and then travel to Philly? Or should they go straight to Philadelphia?

Coach Arbour, along with Torrey and their staff made the call to go home first. But there was a problem. They arrived at one airport and the team bus was at a completely different airport! By this time everybody just wanted to get a couple hours of shuteye. But their long night -- and morning -- was about to get a little longer.

Eventually, they did make it home, before traveling to Philadelphia. But there was no doubt the Islanders were a tired team. And while New York did push the Flyers to a seventh game, that was as far as they got as the Flyers won 5-1 and knocked out the weary Islanders.

From there, there was plenty of turnover over the course of the next few years as players, coaches, management and even ownership all went through some personnel changes.

But come the 1992-93 season, the Isles were looking to get back to the top of the mountain.

After missing the playoffs in back-to-back years for the first time since the first two seasons in franchise history, Bill Torrey stepped down, some would say he was forced out and Don Maloney took over. So it was, the 1992-93 campaign would be the Isles first without Torrey at the helm.

With a respectable 87-points, the Islanders went into the playoffs far from the favorites, but also far from being pushovers.

First came the Capitals, who the Isles dispatched in six-games. It should be noted; the Islanders won Games 2, 3 and 4 all in overtime, with 2 and 4 going to double-overtime.

Then came a date with the two-time defending Cup-Champion Penguins.

The Pens were heavily favored, but somehow the Isles forced a Game 7 and it was in Game 7 that they pulled off one of the most awe inspiring upsets in NHL history.

Even though Pittsburgh opened the scoring, the Isles were not deterred. They even grabbed a 3-1 that they carried late into the third period. But goals by Ron Francis and Rick Tocchet tied the game and forced overtime.

Remember, the Penguins were still heavy favorites to win their third-straight Cup and they had all the momentum on their side after scoring two-goals late in the third period.

Unfortunately for the Penguins, the Islanders had other plans.

First-round playoff hero, Ray Ferraro set-up David Volek for the overtime-winning, series-clinching goal at 5:16 of the first overtime, eliminating the Penguins and sending the Islanders to the Conference Final.

New York fell short against Montreal in the Conference Final but it was the win over Pittsburgh that will always stand out in people's memories.

From there the Islanders were swept out of the playoffs in 1994 by the Rangers and then they didn't see playoff hockey again until the 2001-02 season.

During the "Dark Years" the Isles went through five different Head Coaches, a couple of different jerseys and even got caught up in a scandal when Pickett attempted to sell the team to a Dallas businessman by the name of John Spano.

Considering this is an area in Isles history that most fans would like to forget, I'll just say this; Spano did not have the financial means to own the team and after much back-and-forth was forced to relinquish control back to Pickett. And Spano then got caught up in further fraud scandals, several of which have landed him intermittently in jail over the years. Although, if the records are correct, as of January 2020 he is currently out of jail.

Eventually, a group led by Howard Milstein and Steven Gluckstern bought the team from Pickett. But they didn't last long as they sold the team to Charles Wang after a short term.

Getting back to the on-ice product, the Isles experienced a revival of sorts under Wang's ownership and qualified for the 2002 playoffs where they faced the Maple Leafs in one of the most hostile series in recent history.

The two teams clearly did not get along and that was further exacerbated by the physicality displayed by the Leafs. Although, the Isles did get a few "punches" in, mainly in the form of a Shawn Bates game-winning penalty-shot late in Game 4 that tied the series at two-games apiece.

The Leafs weren't standing for that though and in Game 5, Gary Roberts and Darcy Tucker intentionally -- we don't really know why -- injured the Isles' Kenny Jonsson and captain Michael Peca; effectively ruining the Isles' chances at winning the series.

But the Islanders didn't take that laying down and actually won Game 6 at home by the score of 5-3 to force Game 7. Granted, Game 6 was probably one of the ugliest games you would ever see, as the amount of violence displayed by both teams was unheard of for the current era of hockey. It even featured SIX FIGHTING MAJORS.

However, that was the last gasp for the Islanders as they fell in Game 7. And while they returned to the playoffs several times over the next decade or so, they did not manage to win a single playoff series until they bested the Florida Panthers in the first-round of the 2015-16 playoffs; a full 23-years since their last playoff series victory.

Of course, even without playoff series victories, they still had a few memorable moments, the most prominent of which was Al Arbour's one-game return to the bench as Head Coach during the 2007-08 season.

During the summer of 2007, then Isles Bench Boss Ted Nolan noticed that Arbour was sitting on 1,499 career games as a Head Coach. And while 1,500 wasn't necessarily a record or anything, it was a nice round number and Nolan persuaded Arbour to return for one-game to reach the 1,500 games plateau.

Arbour graciously accepted and on November 3, 2007, he "led" the Islanders to nostalgia-filled, 3-2 win over the Penguins; thus bringing his wins total to 740 (also a nice round number).

Eventually, over the following years, the Islanders began to build a new core of players around the likes of Josh Bailey, John Tavares, Calvin de Haan, Casey Cizikas and current Isles captain, Anders Lee.

And during that time, Wang sold the team to a group led by Scott Malkin and Jon Ledecky. The team even moved to Barclays Center in Brooklyn, New York starting with the 2015-16 season; leaving Nassau Coliseum behind for what it thought would be greener pastures.

While those "greener pastures" did include a playoff series victory over the aforementioned Panthers, the Isles eventually constructed plans to build their own, brand-new arena in Belmont Park, which should be open in time for the 2021-22 season.

But in the meantime, the team currently splits its time between Barclays Center and Nassau Coliseum while it awaits its new home. And while they wait, they continue to win as the second-year tandem of GM Lou Lamoriello and Head Coach Barry Trotz overseas what they hope will be the next great era in Islanders history.

Meanwhile, while we wait for the next great era to come, it's important to remember the previous eras in the franchise's illustrious history. And it is through the eyes of: Neil Best, Greg Bouris, Larry Brooks, Frank Brown, Brendan Burke, Pat Calabria, Hawley Chester III, Brian Compton, Eric Compton, Stan Fischler, Alan Hahn, Shannon Hogan, Chris King, Allan Kreda, Steve Mears, Barry Meisel, Bobby Nystrom, Glenn "Chico" Resch, Howie Rose, Neil Smith, Arthur Staple, John Sterling, Rich Torrey, Ed Westfall and Alyse Zwick that I bring these -- and other -- unforgettable Islanders moments to life.

Buckle up and enjoy the ride down memory lane!

1 NEIL BEST (NEWSDAY)
"GOOD-BYE" TO THE COLISEUM (@NASSAU COLISEUM)
APRIL 11, 2015
NYI 4, CBJ 5 (SO)

BACKGROUND

In sports, it's always important to have versatility. And that is especially true in hockey, where it always seems like a player gets caught out of position at *just* the wrong time and somehow has to try and make the best of the situation.

Well, it's not just the players, who have to be versatile, but the writers and broadcasters too. For you see, something always seems to come up and a reporter who doesn't normally cover a particular team has to all of a sudden go cover a game or event in which he or she normally would not.

Sometimes, it's not even a sport that reporter is used to covering. But they do their best to bring the fans -- readers -- a delectable tale.

In basketball that type of versatility is crucial for the "Sixth Man" on the roster. It's so important that the NBA even has an award for it.

In baseball, GMs and coaches love having what they call, "utility players," a player who can fill-in at multiple positions at the drop of a hat.

Even in hockey you might get a player who can play both offense and defense, who the coach switches back-and-forth depending on the flow of the game.

And while there is no official name in the press box for a reporter who swings from one team to the next -- although some might argue that it's called a General Assignment Reporter -- it is still crucial to a publication's success to have a few versatile reporters on staff.

Of course, one of the best to do this is none other than *Newsday's* own, Neil Best, who likes to call it "parachuting in."

And over the decades -- he's been a mainstay in various New York and New Jersey press boxes for parts of five different decades -- Best has "parachuted in" to cover his fair share of Islanders games.

But how did this transplanted Long Islander end up covering Long Island's favorite team? Read on to find out.

BEST: "Newsday was my hometown paper, even though I lived in New Jersey until I was 11. My junior high and high school were on Long Island. So Newsday was the first paper I really paid attention to. As far as being a sportswriter, the people who knew me, my family and friends when I was in high school, if you would have asked them to guess what I would do, that's what they would have said I would do. But at the time I wasn't thinking necessarily in those terms.

"It wasn't some dream job of mine since childhood. It was just sort of logical. In college I wrote for the college paper, but only occasionally did sports stuff. And even after graduating, it wasn't like I was committed to being a sportswriter. I just sort of needed a job and it made sense.

"In terms of getting into this business, it was mostly because I had no other marketable skills. After college I was working part-time at *Newsday,* in '82, just taking down high school scores on the phone. And then, I went to Anchorage, Alaska, for two-years. It was my first full-time job. I just answered an ad for *Editor and Publisher Magazine.* They liked me, I think partly because I was a part-timer at *Newsday* and partly because I knew about hockey in general and college hockey in particular from going to Cornell and being a big college hockey person.

"That was the most important beat in Anchorage, covering the University of Alaska, Anchorage hockey. So I went up there and then I came back to *Newsday* as a part-timer, covering high schools in the city, in the summer of '85 and I've been there ever since.

"Over the years, at *Newsday,* even though I've never been a hockey beat writer, I was high schools, then I was college basketball, then I was the Giants and then I was the media stuff, all throughout that time I would periodically do hockey. I mean, I did hockey as far back as the winter of '87-'88, when Helene Elliott, our Rangers writer, went to Calgary for the Olympics. I guess I had just become a full-timer by that point, but they sent me to some Rangers stuff.

"I remember I was at Brian Leetch's first practice when he came back from Calgary because Helene was still there. So they (*Newsday*) sent me to Rye Playland to talk to a young Brian Leetch. And over the

2

years I also did Islanders stuff, usually like in the playoffs when they needed extra people to pitch in.

"But in recent years, they've increasingly had me help out with the Islanders and Rangers in the playoffs. And now, with Mark Herrmann, who was sort of our unofficial Islanders columnists taking a buyout this past summer, I guess I'm now the unofficial Islanders and Rangers columnist, but especially the Islanders. We do more columns on them during the regular season. If they keep winning, I think I'll keep being sent to Islanders games."

MOST UNFORGETTABLE ISLANDERS GAME

Since 1972, Nassau Coliseum has meant the world to Islanders fans. It was a home away from home, a place where, for several hours at a time, you could let your hair down, unbutton your tie and chug a beer with 16,000-plus passionate fans; all while rooting for your hometown New York Islanders.

Throughout the course of the franchise's history, The Coliseum, or The Old Barn as it is affectionately known as, was the only place the Islanders ever called home. And like a child growing up, you never want to leave the place you called home.

But, on October 24, 2012, like a parent who has to break the news to their kids, the Islanders announced that after several failed attempts to get what they wanted in regards to a new arena, the team was packing its bags and moving from Uniondale to Brooklyn; from Nassau Coliseum to Barclays Center. And the move would take place at the start of the 2015-16 season.

So, like a child who just got the heartbreaking news, the Islanders fan base was hurt. And since the move was still three-seasons away, it felt like a ticking clock had been positioned over the heads of the franchise and its fans; a countdown to something many wanted no part of.

Yes, The Coliseum was badly in need of an upgrade. Yes, the team was lagging behind in revenue because of the lack of luxury boxes in The Coliseum. But, just like a kid who throws out a toy to only realize after the fact that they want it back, Islanders fans were no longer complaining about The Coliseum, they just wanted to stay.

When the 2014-15 season finally came along, the team decided to honor its past and what the arena had meant to it by spreading out the celebrations throughout the season. But the clock was still ticking and midnight was about to strike.

3

So, even though the team was indeed playoff-bound, guaranteeing at least a couple more games at The Coliseum, the season-finale against the Columbus Blue Jackets on April 11, 2015, felt like a true send-off. And amongst the media contingent in attendance was *Newsday's* Neil Best. So, before I get into the on-ice action, here's what Best had to say about the game.

BEST: "In terms of covering an Islanders game, the most memorable one, it's kind of weird, because in retrospect it turned out to be meaningless, but I covered what we thought was the last game at The Coliseum. And that had a lot of meaning. Even though I was a Rangers fan, as a kid, I was also a Long Islander and I lived through all the Cup-winners and all of that.

"I talked to Jiggs McDonald before the game and it was kind of weird, because at the time, it meant a lot to me to be there for that moment, having someone with the memories I have of going to Islanders games. So it should have been a big moment in history, but looking back now, I guess it wasn't. And I also went to the first game in Brooklyn.

"Now again, that seemed, at the time, like a historic moment, because I was thinking, 'this is the beginning of the next 100-years (for the Islanders), playing in Brooklyn.' I was like, 'it's kind of cool that I'm here.' And I remember thinking that they actually made less of a big deal about it than I thought they would before the opening face-off.

"The announcement in 2012 at Barclays (Center) when the Mayor was there and the Commissioner and they first announced the team was moving to Brooklyn, it seemed like a very historic occasion. It was like, 'wow, this is real.' I mean, it took like two-and-a-half to three-years to actually leave, but it felt like a big deal.

"Just talking to Jiggs before that game when he was standing right next to the Zamboni entrance was kind of cool for me as someone who would listen to him (as a kid). And he obviously meant something to older Islanders fans, at least. I think everybody, all the players at the time, recognized what a big deal this was and most people were not thrilled with it.

"And that turned out to have implications in the future. Looking back on it, the whole build up to that game and what The Coliseum meant to people, it illustrated the ties to The Coliseum that eventually caused, or helped to grease the skids to come back, because everybody kind of realized that something felt off about this Brooklyn thing. History now shows everyone felt that way and that led to the (brief) comeback to The Coliseum.

"It was a weird atmosphere because it was one of those things where it's like a funeral and you're kind of celebrating the person's life, but obviously you're also sad. I think that was kind of the mixture of feelings that day. (In my article) I tried to convey that, because I thought they'd never be back in The Coliseum again.

"(The fans) stated in an emotional way what the place meant to them, how they would miss it and how a lot of people were saying they were never going to go to Brooklyn; which I guess is what turned out to be the case. It illustrated what the arena meant to the team's history. Obviously, if you have a team that wins four-straight Stanley Cups, it doesn't matter where they play, because people are going to remember them fondly anyway. So the arena is kind of a secondary character in these dramas.

"But in this particular case, I think people legitimately thought it contributed to the Islanders' success. Even today, it's obviously a better place to just sit and watch a hockey game than most NHL arenas. And I think there's no question, in real time, in the early-80s, people thought the arena was helping the team; even though, in that era, it obviously wasn't as antiquated as it is now.

"They (the Islanders) had some ceremonies during the course of the season, kind of celebrating (The Coliseum). I think they tried to spread it out a little bit. But that day in particular, I don't think they overdid it, because the team was in a weird spot. They certainly wanted to celebrate The Coliseum, but they also wanted people to be excited about moving to Brooklyn.

"You had this double-edge thing going on. It was just kind of a game. I think for the fans, the game was secondary and it was like a melancholy kind of feeling.

"When they (the Islanders players) were asked about it -- throughout the whole season -- they tried to be good soldiers, good company men, in terms of being positive about the move to Brooklyn. But, they were all pretty honest at the time, starting with (John) Tavares, about how much they'd missed The Coliseum.

"Also, there was the uncertainty over the logistics of the move to Brooklyn, which turned out to be a huge problem, in terms of morning skates and stuff like that. So they were giving respect to The Coliseum, but they also didn't want to come off like they were whining about the Brooklyn thing."

Thank you Neil Best for setting in motion the emotional roller coaster that the game ended up being.

If ever the fans wanted ONE. MORE. WIN. It was in this game. And they brought the energy right out of the gate.

Brock Nelson got the old heart rate up when he broke in all alone on Columbus goalie Curtis McElhinney, but it was all for not as Nelson's shot hit the post. But the Islanders kept coming at McElhinney. However, he stopped all 20 first period shots they sent his way.

Normally, a hot goalie for the visitors might ruin the energy level of the hometown crowd, but the Isles Faithful were not to be deterred. And they let loose when Eric Boulton fought Columbus' Dalton Prout late in the first.

Unfortunately, the home team couldn't capitalize on the raucous energy and even surrendered a goalie to Cam Atkinson with just 10 seconds remaining in the opening period.

There was a nervous energy in the air as the second period started and McElhinney continued to stonewall the Isles, that is, until Kyle Okposo scored at 11:02 of the second to tie the game at 1.

A tie game going into the third period had the fans on the edge of their seats. And, eventually, they were standing and hollering in joy as Boulton and Tavares scored 55 seconds apart early in the third to give the Isles a 3-1 lead. For much of the next six-minutes the fans were excited about the possibility of such an emotional victory.

But then Columbus buckled down and the game changed. At 9:37 of the third Brandon Dubinsky scored to bring The Jackets within 3-2. And his teammate, Alexander Wennberg completed the momentum shift under two-minutes later when he scored to tie the game at 3.

Not to be outdone, the Islanders took back the lead when Nikolay Kulemin scored on a tap-in at 15:36 to get the crowd roaring again. But just as it looked like the Islanders would get the win, Scott Hartnell scored a gut-wrenching goal with just 1:35 remaining in regulation to quiet the crowd and send the game to overtime.

From there overtime bled into the shootout. To start the glorified skills contest John Tavares scored to put the Isles in the lead. But unsuccessful attempts by Okposo and Kulemin gave the Blue Jackets a chance to get back in the game; which they did. A do-or-die goal in Round-Three by Wenneberg necessitated an extra round and after Cal Clutterbuck was turned aside, Atkinson finished what he had started and scored to send the Isles to an emotional 5-4 loss.

So, while the team and its fans didn't get the storybook ending they had hoped for, it was still a game that tugged at the heartstrings of Islanders supporters everywhere. At least until they undid everything with a return to The Coliseum in 2018.

A PICTURE IS WORTH 1,000 WORDS

BEST: "I would say the first time they (*Newsday*) sent me to an Islanders game at The Coliseum, in the late-80's. Like I said, I was helping with the Rangers when Helene was in Calgary. So, they would also occasionally send me to help with Islanders games. I'm not talking about a specific game, but for me, as someone who grew up in that Cup era, I mean, we moved to Long Island a month before the Islanders played their first game ever.

"So, I kind of grew up with that franchise as someone who moved to Long Island from New Jersey. The first time I covered a game at The Coliseum in that press box, which looks basically exactly the same today with the little stairway up to the room with the hotdogs. It all looks exactly the same today, even after the renovation. The first time I went in there and saw all of the hockey writers. I saw the setup itself.

"I saw what is still one of the best views of the ice in the NHL, because it's so up close, even though it's high. To see all the hockey writers of that era, like *Newsday's* Pat Calabria. And back then, all the papers covered the Islanders, unlike today. Just to see that place, all those writers and the buzz around The Coliseum after seeing it on television all those years, because, like I said, I'd gone to a couple of games as a fan in The Cup era, but this was my first time as a writer and that was very cool.

"I mean, I was in my late-20's, I was a hockey guy and I had read all those hockey writers through the glory days. And just to see it, to be there, was like, 'wow, okay, this is pretty cool.' And I still think about that when I go there now. It hasn't changed. The Garden is completely different, even though it's the same building. The Coliseum, it's the same. I mean, it is exactly the same with maybe some new carpeting or something.

"It is now 30-plus years since the first time I covered a game there and that's what I remember. I know it's not on the ice, but I just know it was very cool just to be around the hockey writers from that era. I mean, hockey still matters, obviously and we still cover it, but it had a different feeling then.

"There was a time in the '70's where people thought the NHL was going to surpass the NBA in popularity because the NBA was having a lot of problems in the pre-Jordan/Bird/Magic era. That was actually a thing. People thought hockey was going to surpass basketball and become the Number Three sport. So it just seemed bigger in terms of the general sports fan world than it does today. It all just seemed very big to me. Plus I was in my 20's, so of course I was more easily impressed than I am now."

2 GREG BOURIS (ISLANDERS PR)
HOW LONG CAN THEY GO? THE EASTER EPIC
(@CAPITAL CENTER)
APRIL 18, 1987
NYI 3, WSH 2 (4OT)

BACKGROUND

The sports industry is a difficult nut to crack, even for the most qualified candidates. Unless you are a top-notch athlete, or you have some important connection to a top-tier executive, you are going to be amongst an applicant pool that ranges in the thousands for even the most basic of jobs.

Knowing this, many would get discouraged and try their luck in another field. But there are some who won't be deterred and it is those few who often go on to have extraordinary success in the industry.

There is a lot of scratching and clawing to get a foot in the door and even more scratching and clawing to get beyond the entrance way. But as you begin to move further into the room, you'll find that the potential for success is unlimited. And that's where the story of Greg Bouris, a young man from Pawtucket, Rhode Island, begins.

Bouris, who grew up loving all sports, refused to let any obstacle beat him. And over time, that determination led him to ascend to the top of the Islanders Public Relations department; all at the tender age of 26 no less.

It's quite an interesting yarn and one that Bouris enjoys sharing. So let's delve right in.

BOURIS: "I grew up in Pawtucket, Rhode Island, just about an hour South of Boston, Massachusetts. We (my family and I) were kind of in that New England sports realm and I was a big sports fan growing up. I loved all sports and followed all teams. When it came time to make a decision, after high school, what I was going to do, I applied to college (to URI), was accepted and then received the bill for my first tuition payment and didn't really understand how I was gonna pay for it.

"My parents were divorced. They had very little means to put me through college. So, despite being accepted to URI, I said, 'Well, I can't afford to go to college, so I'm going to get a job like everybody else.' And Pawtucket was a very industrial area, although it's changed now. But back then, there were still quite a few factories around. So, the low hanging fruit for somebody 18-years-old, to get a job, was to get a factory job.

"I got a job in a factory down the end of my street. The name of the company was E.F. Rosen and they were a candy company. They made a lot of novelty candies, and I became the floor boy on the lollipop floor, schlepping pallets of lollipops down to the trucks and shipping them all around the world. It didn't take long for me to be doing the kind of work where I realized that I should really rethink the college piece.

"This was in the late-70's to early-80's, as I graduated in 1978 from high school. It was clearly pre-internet age. So information wasn't as accessible back then. I didn't really know much. Nobody in my family had gone to college directly, so the process was a little foreign. But long story short, I found my way to Rhode Island Junior College and the tuition there was about $250 a semester.

"I could swing that by getting a job, so I did. I had a job at a local hospital in Providence and began taking courses at the junior college. After three semesters, because I missed the equivalent of what would've been the first semester of my freshman year, I wanted to start at a four-year school in September. I didn't want to wait to graduate with an Associates Degree and again start in the middle of the year.

"I wanted to go to a college. I went to meet with my advisor and she asked, 'Well, what are you interested in?' I said, 'Well, I like business. But I love sports and aren't sports businesses?' She said, 'Well they kind of are, so it makes sense that maybe there is a way to combine a business degree with an opportunity in sports. So, let's do some digging.'

"In whatever manuals and guidebooks they had in the late-70's, we came across a college in Miami, in North Miami, called Biscayne College, which today is St. Thomas University. About two years prior, they became, I believe, the first college to offer an undergraduate degree in what's known as Sports Administration; specifically its own program and department. We sent away for some information and they sent it back.

"It was exactly what I was looking for. So I applied to Biscayne College, was accepted and received some financial aid, given my parents' economic status and other things. From there, I went down to Miami and I fell in love with the academic work, mixing the business courses with sports courses. And the thing with being in Miami at that particular time, on campus, the Miami Dolphins trained there.

"So we were in this NFL atmosphere with Don Shula, Bob Griese and that whole late-70's group of Dolphins. The (Baltimore) Orioles also used that as their home spring training base. So, the culture and environment was conducive to what we were studying. Our Athletic Director was also the basketball coach, Ken Stabler, and he had played (when he was in College). We were a Division-II school, but we played and scheduled probably about four or five Division-I teams a year.

"A couple of them would be at the little high school gym of the junior college down the road. We played Houston in Texas and I had my college work-study job in the athletic department. So that kind of got me off and running. As a New Englander, I didn't like the weather in South Florida, so I did a little more research while I was down there and found that UMass Amherst also had a PR program similar to the sports administration program.

"That was a bit harder to find because, at the time, it was in their Phys-Ed department and it was in their department of sports studies with a sports management focus. So I applied to UMass to transfer and was accepted. It was the same thing (as with in Miami), a great program, a great offering and a bigger school.

"So, I had a lot more to choose from in terms of other courses that could supplement my background and what my interests were. From there, part of the requirement was, before you graduated, you had to do an internship. It was a requirement and a lot of the graduate students ahead of us and some of the undergrads; they were looking to do internships at tennis centers as those facilities were just popping up. A lot of people were focused on facility management and they wanted to go that route.

"A lot of people were focused on the NFL, the NBA or the MLB; nobody was really talking about hockey. And I thought, 'maybe that's my in to get an internship where I won't be competing with others for that spot.' So, I talked to my advisor and UMass had had an intern the year before at the NHL. He (my advisor) made the phone call to the NHL to see if they would be interested in another UMass student for an internship and they said, 'yes, have him (me) come in for an interview.'

"It was the first time I'd ever gone to New York and it was for that interview, which ended with me being offered the internship at the

NHL office in Midtown. At that point, they were at 1221 Avenue of the Americas.

"Needless to say, we're talking about 1983. The industry hardly even resembles what it is today. There may have been 25 employees at the league level back then. Today, there are probably 200 employees, if not more.

"So I packed my bags and lived with a buddy of mine from Providence, who I knew from the hospital that I worked at, who was going to school at Fordham. My internship was without pay, it was for credit and they only gave me commuting costs each day. I believe the subway was like 90 cents at that time.

"I think I got paid $1.80 a day, but I was happy to be in the big city and working at the NHL doing a lot of public relations and marketing support. At that same time, John Halligan, the late-John Halligan, who was the longtime PR Director for the Rangers, he came over to the league as the Vice President of Communications.

"He connected me with the VP of Public Relations for the Knicks and so, I was able to secure a game night position with the Knicks. So, in addition to my $1.80 a day, I was then making about $25-$30 a game working for the Knicks. I managed to put a little more food on my plate, macaroni and cheese or whatever. But I got further involved and entrenched in the New York sports scene and learned from some very experienced people.

"When my internship with the NHL ended after its' 15-week duration the NHL offered me to stay on for the rest of the season. It wasn't a full-time job, but it was with higher pay -- an hourly rate. That was the 1983-84 season and it was towards the end of the Islanders run. That was the year of their 'Drive for Five.' They were kind of the preeminent franchise in America at the time. And so, after my internship concluded -- after the Stanley Cup in '84, when the Oilers beat the Islanders -- I packed my bags and moved back to Rhode Island.

"We didn't have email back then, so, through research and snail mail I sent out resumes to a whole slew of professional sports organizations, looking for work, for my first real full-time job.

"Long story short, the Publicity Assistant of the New York Islanders, the third person on the three-person staff was leaving to take a different position. So that job opened up and John Halligan reached out to me and said, 'Hey, there's going to be this opening, are you interested? I said, 'of course.' So they sent my resume over to the Islanders.

"The Islanders invited me in for an interview. I went down to Long Island, interviewed for the position and was offered the position beginning just before Training Camp launched in 1984. I joined the

Islanders as a Publicity Assistant in '84-'85 and I was promoted to Publicity Director in '86. I was 26 and at the time and I believe I was the youngest PR Director in all of professional sports."

MOST UNFORGETTABLE ISLANDERS GAME

When the Islanders were swept out of the playoffs in 1986 by the Capitals it looked like a changing of the guard was underway, as the Caps had finally gotten past the Isles after several failed attempts. In fact, that sweep even -- partially -- led to a change on the Isles' bench as longtime Head Coach Al Arbour chose to step down from his post.

So by the time the 1986-87 playoffs got underway and the Isles and Caps once again found themselves matched up with one another, it was fair to wonder if New York could reclaim its crown of superiority.

Well, the early answer was 'No,' as Washington went up 3-1 in the series and had the Islanders one loss away from back-to-back way-too-early playoff exits.

But fear not Islanders fans, for your team still had some semblance of past class, when it was the four-time, reigning, defending, Stanley Cup champion of the NHL. And thanks to that past class, the Islanders stormed back in the series to force a Game 7 on the night before Easter Sunday down in Washington D.C.

BOURIS: "The Capitals had some great, great teams. The fact was, the way the playoff format ran, they had to run through the Islanders to get out of the Patrick division and get to the Semi-Finals. And they never could overcome that hurdle. They thought in '87 they finally had the Islanders where they wanted them. We (the Islanders) lost to the Caps the year before in a short series. So, I think they thought that maybe the tide had finally turned and they had down three-games-to-one. But we chipped away, forced Game 7, went back down to Washington and the rest is history."

Heading into Game 7 the Isles had the all-important momentum on their side and they knew they were going to need it to come out on top.

BOURIS: "There was a lot of nervous energy in the room. I think the players felt confident, but not overly confident; Al would never let them get that way. This was a group of champions walking in here. They knew what had to be done and I got the sense from the other side, the Caps people, they were nervous."

The game started fast and furious as the shots flew from both sides, but neither goalie gave an inch, that is, until the 19:12 mark of the first period when Capitals forward Mike Gartner put the puck past Isles netminder Kelly Hrudey for the 1-0 lead.

In a game like this a 1-0 lead or conversely, a 1-0 deficit, felt much bigger than it actually was. But that is what happens in Game 7's. Any goal at any time can be the deciding score. So, going into the second period, it was Washington who now had all the momentum.

However, these Islanders still carried around a fragment of their championship gene from yesteryear and at the 11:35 mark of the second period, Pat Flatley tied the game by putting one past Caps goalie Bob Mason.

Now the pressure was really on. Half the game was gone and neither team was ready to go home for the summer. And as they say in hockey, desperation is key.

Well, the Capitals expressed their desperation the only way they knew how, by scoring, as Grant Martin put them back in front at the 18:45 mark of the second period; thus leaving the Islanders with just a drop over 21-minutes to either score another goal or call it a season.

The Isles chose Option 1, as Bryan Trottier scored the game-tying goal with just 5:23 to go in the third period; thereby crushing Washington's spirit or so he hoped.

And as the final five-minutes-and-change ticked off the clock it became apparent that this game was going to be decided in overtime. After all, why stop at just three periods of regulation? A game of this magnitude clearly needed more.

BOURIS: "It was a remarkable game. And the funny thing is, the one thing I remember the most was sitting through the game in the press box and then going down in-between periods in my role as PR Director and I was confident (we were going to win). I had this eerie confidence that I didn't care if the game went another minute or another 10-hours, we were going to win the game. I just kind of had that feeling."

Bouris' confidence was admirable, but there was no way of knowing which team would be the last one standing as the game headed into the first overtime period.

And from there, one overtime became two, which became three and eventually four; which put it in the NHL's record book as one of the longest games in history. Of course, the game didn't get to a fourth-overtime by accident. The goalies, Kelly Hrudey and Bob Mason were just that good.

BOURIS: "Kelly Hrudey was terrific. Again, the game wasn't defensive-minded at the time. I think, between the two teams, those goalies made over 120 combined saves, which is remarkable. Kelly had 73-saves. And some of those were breakaways and two-on-one odd man rushes. I clearly remember Kelly just kind of standing on his head. He was seeing the puck as if it was a beach ball. And I remember with every one of those saves you just kind of got the feeling that the Caps just got a little more deflated."

If Hrudey's saves got the Caps "just a little deflated," you can just imagine how they felt when Pat LaFontaine scored the game-winning, series-clinching goal.

BOURIS: "The game ended at like 2 o'clock in the morning on Pat LaFontaine's turnaround, blind shot into the net. Everybody was relieved. Pat was jumping up and down. The rest of the players were kind of holding him down like, 'stop, we can't jump up and down. We have no energy left.'"

So, while the Islanders had secured yet another impressive playoff series victory, they still had work to do. And that work began with what to do next.

BOURIS: "Getting home there's actually a funny story. Being there, by the time we got home, there were decisions to make now that we were moving on to play the Flyers. The decision that Al Arbour, Bill Torrey and the training staff were trying to make was, right after the game, 'what do we do now? Do we go to Philly or do we go home?'

"The decision was to fly home, because, the trainer, Craig Smith, felt that the guys who needed treatment, he'd rather treat them at The Coliseum and then we could get down there. It was a short bus ride, so Al said, 'yeah, that makes sense. Let the guys go home and sleep. Anybody who needs treatment can get treatment and then we'll all be back at The Coliseum at like 5 o'clock for the bus ride down to Philly.'

"So, now we knew what we were doing. And by the time we got home, the sun was coming up. Now, we always flew in and out of LaGuardia, which is where the charters were. But they were closed so we couldn't land in LaGuardia.

"We had to land at JFK. So we landed at JFK and it may have been like 6 in the morning. But nobody told the bus driver that we were going to be at JFK. So he was waiting at LaGuardia and when we landed at JFK, there was no bus. We had to wait for the bus driver to get to us. So, that long trip became even longer.

"Eventually, we got on the bus and then we got to The Coliseum and there were hundreds of people out there with big signs, saying things like, 'The Never Say Die-Islanders.' And that sort of became the mantra.

"Then everybody went home and tried to get some sleep. But I couldn't really get any sleep because my phone was ringing like crazy from the media once they woke up and saw what was going on. There was the whole, 'hey we want to tell the behind the scenes story of what's going on.' So, you try to do what you can do, but I also had to protect the players in terms of, 'hey, we've still got another round to play, so we've got to get going.'

"We did some media things but not too much, because we had to get back to The Coliseum, get on the bus and get to Philadelphia. I think we played fairly well that first game, but we ended up losing the series after falling behind in that series three-games-to-one. Then the same thing happened. We came back to tie it 3-3 but, unfortunately, we had to go down to Philly to The Spectrum, the hostile Spectrum for the seventh game against the Flyers. They jumped us pretty fast I remember and they won the game. But it was a pretty amazing ride."

A PICTURE IS WORTH 1,000 WORDS

BOURIS: "The one thing that sticks in my mind is a photo op I put together. It was the day we traded Brent Sutter and Pat LaFontaine. (They were packaged in two separate trades). It was a huge day, especially in what I had to do in public relations. On that day we moved: Brent Sutter, Brad Lauer, Randy Wood, Pat LaFontaine, Randy Hillier and a fourth-round draft pick in the 1992 Draft. And we brought back: Pierre Turgeon, Benoit Hogue, Dave McLlwaine, Uwe Krupp, Adam Creighton and Steve Thomas. We brought back like six players and it was total mayhem because we had traded the star of the team; Pat LaFontaine.

"It was kind of the ending of a contract dispute he was having with the organization. And that was challenging, because I liked Pat. We came in at the same time. (Patrick) Flatley, LaFontaine and myself, we all came in around the same time.

"I was very good friends with Pat, but at the end of the day, I had a job to do too. During that contract dispute I had to park my friendship with Pat and do what I had to do for the organization.

"But on the day of that trade, I remember a couple of funny things.

"Uwe Krupp was, at the time, the tallest player in the NHL and the trade happened so fast that they didn't have a Jersey that would fit him. So they had to cut the bottom off of one Islander jersey to sew it onto the bottom of another one. They cut the stripes off of one and then cut a longer piece off another jersey and sewed that together so he had a jersey long enough to wear in the game.

"And just before, or after, warm-ups I gathered the photographers: *the AP* photographer and maybe the *Newsday* photographer. I have a black and white image of it, I believe. I had them all stand out there in a line before they went out; all the newcomers. So that is the picture I have in my mind."

3 LARRY BROOKS (NY POST)
MIKE BOSSY 50 GOALS IN 50 GAMES (@ NASSAU COLISEUM)
JANUARY 24, 1981
NYI 7, QUE 4

BACKGROUND

There is an old saying that something is, "As American as apple pie."

And while hockey is not necessarily an American sport, it certainly has a lot of history in the United States of America.

Of course, not every state or city has an NHL team, but there are also some, like New York, that have multiple teams.

And with the abundance of teams in New York -- the Buffalo Sabres, New York Islanders and New York Rangers -- there are also a good number of writers who are tasked with covering each team.

For some, these writers are viewed as the guardians of their team's history. Now, not every writer is viewed this way. But there are an exceptional few who have been around long enough to have truly earned the right to be guardians of a team's history.

In New York, we have been blessed to have several writers over the generations who have been as much a part of a team or teams' history as the players themselves.

And one writer in particular, who is currently in his sixth decade covering the New York sports scene, has earned the right to be a part of the history of the teams he has covered.

That writer is Larry Brooks. And for decades there has been nothing to define New York sports coverage as much as opening a copy of the New York Post, turning to the sports section and reading Brooks' latest article or column.

For fans who equate Brooks' coverage with only the Rangers, you might want to continue reading, as he has covered a lot more than just the Blueshirts. In fact, he was actually an Islanders writer long before he ever started covering the Rangers. And that's where his Hall of Fame career began.

In 2018, it was an honor for Brooks to learn of his induction into the NHL's Hockey Hall of Fame as a recipient of the prestigious Elmer Ferguson Award and it added a well-deserved feather to his cap. After all, his career at The NY Post began back in 1976.

But how exactly did this generational career come about? And more importantly, in a career that has been spread over parts of six decades, what Islanders games and moments does Brooks consider to be his most unforgettable?

Well, for starters, Larry Brooks grew up on Manhattan's Upper West Side as a huge New York Rangers fan. In fact, he even had season tickets (Section 419). And he continued to support the Blueshirts throughout his high school years at the Bronx High School of Science and his college years at CCNY.

However, once he completed his time at CCNY, the universe decided to throw him a curveball, or rather, a hip-check.

"I got out of school, I majored in Political Science and I was going to go to Law School," said Brooks. "And I didn't. Honestly, I was looking for a job and there was a clerk's job open at The Post. A friend of mine was working as a clerk. He had a job as a clerk at The Post and they were looking for somebody else to come in and work overnights. So in late October, early November of 1975 I started working as a clerk.

"I was working overnight doing agate," continued Brooks. "At that time, reporters dictated their stories into a tape recorder. And I did a lot of transcribing. There were different jobs for a clerk on the overnight. And so I was working there for a few months, a couple of nights a week -- two, three nights a week -- as a voucher employee, part-time guy. And I had a great time. I loved it, going into work overnight, talking about sports, it was great.

"Then in 1976, the summer of '76, the Olympics were in Montreal and the (daytime) sports editor, who I'd never met before, I'd never met anyone at The Post who worked in the daytime, wanted me to come in and work days. We'd sent writers up there and the sports editor wanted me to come in and work days. And I remember actually telling the night guy that I didn't want to and he said, 'no, well the sports editor wants you to work days.' So I went in and I was doing rewrite.

"What would happen is, a guy up there covering would call in during the day because The Post at that time was a PM paper. So we had like three, four, five, six, seven additions during the day and they just kept reprinting the paper with updates during the day. So, the guys covering in Montreal would call in and somebody would be assigned then to write the story for the next edition. So, Paul Zimmerman was up there covering and it was my job to do rewrite. He would call and give the information, then you'd have to write the story and you'd have to get it up pretty quick because the additions ran basically every hour, every hour and a half.

"And I know I'm making a short story long, but I ripped off a couple of stories quickly and the sports editor said to me, right there on the spot, 'who are you and what do you want to do?' So I said, 'well, I want to cover hockey.' And he gave me the job right there to cover the Islanders in '76. So I had worked for a few months as a part time clerk and then I started covering the Islanders."

Talk about doing a complete 180. There was Brooks, a born and bred Rangers fan, covering Islanders games.

BROOKS: "(Covering the Islanders) was my first real job. I covered the Islanders starting with the '76-'77 season.

"It was very beneficial to me that I wasn't assigned to the Rangers. When they asked me what I wanted to do, I said I wanted to cover hockey and they immediately said, 'okay, you're going to have the Islanders.' My first reaction was, 'The Islanders?! I hate the Islanders.'

"But as it developed, covering the Rangers would have been impossible for me. I would have been covering guys who I had grown up rooting for my entire life. I would've just gone from the Blue Seats to covering them. It would not have been an easy transition for me. The Islanders were much different though because they was such a young team and the relationship between the writers and the players back then was so different than it is now.

"Once I got there, it wasn't the Islanders I had spent the last couple of years of my life rooting against. They came into the league in '72, so it's not like I grew up hating the Islanders; there were no Islanders. But it was a group of guys who were eminently likeable, who were very, very good and great to deal with. So, within a very, very short time, my allegiances and fandom fell away.

"Honestly, my allegiance and fandom fell away the minute I was told I was covering the Islanders. It wasn't anything I had to wrestle with. I didn't go there as a fan. I didn't go there thinking as a fan. I went there as somebody wanting to keep my job, because back then, when you were given a promotion, which I was, it was a 90-day probation period. And so, I was just concerned about doing the job well enough that I kept it.

"But covering that team and that group of players, it set the foundation for my career. They were the best couple of years I ever had, both because of the kind of team they were and because of the kinds of guys they were and the kinds of relationships I developed with them; away from the rink, with them and their wives. My fiancé at the time, then wife, we would all go out together, spend time together, socialize together. I was extremely fortunate to get that gig."

MOST UNFORGETTABLE ISLANDERS GAME

When a team like the early-80s New York Islanders comes along, you just have to sit back and wait for something special to happen. And trust me, you wouldn't be waiting for long, because that's how frequent special things happened for those Islanders.

With four Stanley Cups, numerous epic comebacks and several Hall of Fame players to choose from, you could start writing a list of their incredible moments on New Year's Day and not be finished when the following New Year's Eve came around.

But sometimes, an unforgettable moment becomes even more special when there is a personal relationship attached to it. And that was exactly the case when Mike Bossy equaled the legendary "Rocket" Richard by scoring 50-goals in 50 games. For Bossy and *NY Post* beat writer, Larry Brooks, theirs is a relationship that has lasted decades. And other than Bossy and his teammates, it's quite possible that nobody inside Nassau Coliseum was happier to see Bossy equal Richard than Brooks.

BROOKS: "I still talk to Mike every once in awhile. I check in with him. He and (Martin) Brodeur -- and Henrik Lundqvist, who is operating in a different era -- they were the two greatest players I ever covered who were equally great dealing with the writers and dealing with the press. You could talk to them for hours and hours.

"I covered Mike from his rookie season. I covered most of Marty's career. I've covered most of Lundqvist's career, starting with his rookie season and I do think Bossy is my favorite player who I covered in terms of both his performance and our relationship.

"He was a great interview and a great player. His goal scoring sort of overshadowed the fact that he became a great two-way player. His first couple of years, Al (Arbour) used to pull him off the late-game face-offs and Mike was irritated.

"If they were up by a goal late in the game, they might skip his shift. And then, as he evolved as a player, Bossy became one of the best penalty-killers in the NHL and became one of the best defensive players in the NHL.

"You talk about the greatest players ever -- Bossy. (In regards to the 50 in 50) I wanted him to get it. I wanted him to get it for him and I wanted him to get it for the story. It was a huge thing to get 50 in 50. It hadn't been done since Richard."

And it might surprise some of you to read this, but Bossy had actually openly talked about going for 50 in 50 when he was still early in his chase.

BROOKS: "A couple of months earlier Mike Bossy came out and actually said that his goal was to score 50 (goals) in 50 (games). He got off to a great start and he went on the record and said, 'my goal is to score 50-goals in 50-games,' because he wanted to equal Maurice Richard's record. That was extremely important to him.

"I don't exactly remember, but I think I was somewhat taken aback (when Bossy said he wanted to get 50 in 50). But, by that time, I also knew Bossy well and it kind of fit with his personality as a confident and almost cocky type of player. He understood how good he was. He understood who he was and who he was as a player. He was always outspoken, always honest.

"So, he was going at his pace and was ahead of Richard's pace when he had 48-goals in 47-games. And then he was shutout the next two games.

"I remember there was a game in Detroit -- Detroit was Game 49 -- and the Red Wings had, I believe it was Paul Woods on Bossy as a checker. He just followed him the whole game. He did nothing else. He just wanted to keep the puck away from Bossy.

"So they (the Islanders) came back home on a Saturday night and they were playing Quebec. He had 48-goals in 49-games.

"I was doing some freelancing then for *Sports Illustrated* and Charlie Simmer of the Kings had 46-goals in 49-games and the Kings were in Boston for a Saturday afternoon game. *SI* sent me up to Boston to do that game and then I came back to The Coliseum to do the Islanders. So, you had Simmer going for 50 in 50 and Simmer had been under the radar the entire time. It was all Bossy, Bossy, Bossy. And there was Simmer with a chance to do it before Bossy. He (Simmer) scored twice and then he scored an empty-netter and wound up with 49 in 50."

So now it was down to Bossy. Could he get two-goals in his one remaining game? I mean, he had plenty of two-goal games in his career; it would surely be almost routine, right? Not so fast. As Bossy was about to find out, sometimes things aren't as easy as one makes them seem.

BROOKS: "So then, I went to The Coliseum (from Boston) and there were the Islanders and Bossy. He had a brutal game, just a brutal game. The entire focus was on Bossy, that's all anyone cared about. He had a brutal first two periods. I don't know if he had a scoring chance. He was fumbling the puck and they were tight.

"Quebec didn't do the same thing as Detroit, but he was as tight as I'd ever seen him. I remember going to The Coliseum and being certain he was going to score twice. And then it got to the third period and it was like, 'maybe not.'

"He was being shutout until the final five-minutes. Then he scored one with about four, maybe four-and-a-half minutes to go, on the power-play. And I think on either his next shift or two shifts later, at five-on-five, it was a broken play, Quebec was trying to get out of their zone and couldn't.

"There was a turnover and the pass went to Bossy in the left-circle. I think the pass came from Bryan Trottier, a cross-ice pass and Bossy one-timed.

"So, Bossy scored from the left-circle and then he went into this dance on the ice. The bench emptied and the players poured onto the ice. They were hugging him and stuff.

"Everybody came on the ice back then. I think until maybe the '90s, when any sort of milestone goal was scored, the entire team would leave the bench and come onto the ice. It happened all the time. It was one of those things that just stopped. I think a rule might have been put in place.

"(Anyway) it was 50 in 50. It was just, for all The Cup-winning games I saw, the overtimes and double-overtimes, all of their great wins, but from a historical perspective, Bossy getting 50 in 50 was a remarkable feat. Plus there was the fact; he had talked about it so much; that's what also made it remarkable.

"He said after the game that in fact, after the second period, he was embarrassed and he didn't know what he was going to say after the game to explain away the fact that he had failed."

There it was, Mike Bossy had done what no one other than Rocket Richard had done; scoring 50-goals in 50-games. And the roar from The Coliseum crowd showed just how much he meant to the fans.

For Brooks, it was an "interesting day," to cover two attempts, one failed and one successful, at equaling The Rocket. It's just a shame that *SI* didn't run the piece. And as for *The Post*, there was no Sunday paper back then. Oh well, maybe next time.

A PICTURE IS WORTH 1,000 WORDS

BROOKS: "It would be a photo of my wife, me, Bob Bourne and his wife, Clark Gillies and his wife, Dave Lewis and his wife, Lorne Henning and his wife, Billy Harris and Eddie Westfall at Dr. G's, which was a pub about 10-minutes away from The Coliseum that we used to go to after every Saturday night game. We were essentially all the same age. We were friends. There was a line, but we were friends and we'd go out. It's funny, because you'd go out with a group of guys at home and a slightly different group of guys on the road.

"(Mike) Bossy and (Bryan) Trottier never went out. They didn't drink. Bossy and Trottier never went out with the rest of the guys. They went off themselves or they just went back to the hotel or back home after games.

"But the picture of my time with the Islanders would have been going out with them after games because that kind of defined how I grew up covering that team and how I started my career. Players and writers intermingled all the time. So, after a game, when we were on the road, my first question often was, 'where are we going?' It had nothing to do with the game.

"I'd go up to J.P. Parise or Billy Harris or whoever and say, 'where are we going?' I saw a lot of great games and a lot of Cup championships and great players, but that would capture the essence of my experience covering the Islanders."

4 FRANK BROWN (NY DAILY NEWS)
THE EASTER EPIC, ENOUGH SAID! (@CAPITAL CENTER)
APRIL 18, 1987
NYI 3, WSH 2 (4OT)

BACKGROUND

Anytime you can say that somebody is a Hall of Famer, it is quite a big deal. For players, being elected to the Hall of Fame is the pinnacle of one's career; regardless of how many championships you won or records you set.

But it isn't just players who can receive immortal enshrinement in the NHL's Hockey Hall of Fame. Coaches, executives, scouts, owners, broadcasters and writers can also receive this most permanent of honors. And let me tell you, there are far fewer broadcasters and writers in the Hall than there are players, coaches, etc.

So, it means a little something extra to the fine men and women who have spent their careers providing the type of coverage that so often goes unappreciated at the time, when they get that special "Hall Call."

And one such writer to receive "The Call" is none other than Frank Brown, who spent the bulk of his writing career with the *NY Daily News* and was rewarded for it in 2019, as a recipient of the prestigious Elmer Ferguson Memorial Award; which carried immediate induction into the Hall of Fame.

For those of you wondering how such a tremendous career was born, here is Brown himself telling the tale:

BROWN: "At the time, options were severely limited for a passionate hockey fan who wanted to be involved in the sport in any way possible. There were only 12 NHL teams and only so many opportunities to cover them: you were on TV, you were on radio, or you wrote. There was only one NHL team in New York and leaving New York to pursue the dream wasn't in any way a consideration.

"I wasn't going to be able to break into TV or radio; I had no formal training and the people who were broadcasting Rangers games were too good and too entrenched. I figured that if there were any pathway at all, it would be through freelance writing.

"My eighth-grade English teacher, Mrs. Morgan, drilled grammar and language skills into her students. She fostered in me an appreciation for words used well. She energized an interest in reading. And I did pretty well on my writing assignments. Ultimately, I'm not certain whether I chose sports journalism or sports journalism chose me; I am certain it worked out better than I ever could have imagined.

"There are thousands of sports writers who are, or were, just one lucky break away from being able to tell stories to huge audiences in unique, entertaining and powerfully engaging ways. There are writers, likely better ones than I, who never were published by the world's largest news gathering operation (*The Associated Press*) or by what was, at the time, New York's biggest-selling tabloid, *The Daily News*.

"It was one of the great moments in my life to be hired as a 'sports clerk' by *The AP* just as I was starting at Hunter College on Park Avenue in New York City. I could work on a liberal arts degree during the day and an informal, hands-on sports journalism degree – from some of the top professionals in the business – while I did sports department grunt work at night and on weekends.

"When *The AP* hired me in 1970, I told them I happily would do whatever was asked – as long as I was given a chance to 'make the varsity' upon graduation. They agreed to those terms, and, to my astonishment, honored them when I graduated in 1973. I was given a tryout and passed, becoming, at 21 years of age, one of the youngest staff sports writers in modern AP history.

"I had been covering hockey stories fairly frequently, without a byline, as one of the perks of my period as a trainee. Hockey was an outlier sport then; there weren't many folks at AP who were interested in it, understood it or wanted anything to do with it.

"Hal Bock was AP's national hockey writer at the time; if there was an assignment for which Hal wasn't available, I would instantly volunteer. I am almost certain I covered the Islanders' first game at Nassau Coliseum as part of that arrangement. Not long after I was hired, Hal became a national sports columnist and the national hockey writer position came available.

"I leaped at it – which led to more Islanders coverage and another massive bolt-from-the-blue: In 1980, I was assigned to cover hockey at the Olympic Winter Games at Lake Placid. So I covered 'the Miracle.'

"Just a few months later, I was covering the 1980 Stanley Cup Final between the Islanders and Flyers. I was sitting in the pressroom at the Spectrum in Philadelphia before one of the games when a man walked up to me and said, 'Hi. I'm Buddy Martin, sports editor of *the New York Daily News* and I'm going to hire you. I've already talked to your boss.'

"I finished covering the series, and the Islanders' first Stanley Cup, for *The AP*. A few months afterward, I started at *The Daily News*. I had grown up with the Rangers, and had covered a ton of their games for AP. The Rangers were being covered admirably by Lawrie Mifflin, so I was tasked with the Islanders beat and covered their Cups in 1981 and 1982 before moving more to Rangers coverage and ultimately becoming *the Daily News* hockey columnist."

MOST UNFORGETTABLE ISLANDERS GAME

From 1980-1983, no team dominated the NHL more than the New York Islanders. The Boys from Long Island won four-straight Stanley Cups and 19-straight playoff series; feats that will almost definitely never be replicated.

But as they say, all good things must come to an end. And the Edmonton Oilers saw to that in 1984, as they ended the Isles' dreams of a fifth-straight Cup and a 20th-straight series victory; thus kick starting the Oilers' own dynasty.

However, just because the Isles dynasty was over didn't mean that the team had to just suddenly fall apart.

Actually, quite the opposite occurred, as the Islanders continued to be an annual presence in the playoffs. They just weren't going all the way anymore.

Some of their stars moved on, either to other teams or into retirement, but a core group still remained. Mike Bossy, Denis Potvin, Billy Smith and Bryan Trottier all remained with the team as the 1980's chugged along. And of course, they were still led by dual masterminds, Bill Torrey and Al Arbour.

But as the core group continued to age, Torrey decided he needed to retool and thus brought in stars such as; Pat LaFontaine and Kelly Hrudey to hopefully help build towards another Cup-run.

However, following a disappointing opening-round sweep to the Washington Capitals in 1986, Al Arbour decided a change was needed and informed Torrey he was stepping down as the team's Head Coach; a position he had held since 1973.

So, with a new Head Coach in place for the 1986-87 season, there was a different feeling around the team.

Terry Simpson's boys were still a playoff team -- extending the team's streak to 13-consecutive years making the playoffs -- but they were no longer elite. And they faced a daunting task in the opening-round as they once again faced their habitual foes, the Washington Capitals.

The teams traded victories in D.C. before coming back to Nassau Coliseum for Games 3 and 4; both of which were won by the Caps and put the Isles on the brink of elimination heading back to D.C. for Game 5.

Another "way-too-early" first-round exit would have likely led to more personnel changes for the Isles and that was something the team wanted no part of. So, how do you prevent unwanted changes from occurring? Simple, you win. And you win and you win some more.

The Isles won Game 5 4-2 and then went home to rock The Old Barn with a 5-4 win in Game 6 to set-up a "winner-take-all" Game 7 in D.C. on Saturday April 18, 1987, the night before Easter Sunday. A win would send the Islanders to the Division Finals against the Philadelphia Flyers. A loss...well, they didn't want to think about that.

And who would be in attendance to cover the Islanders that night in D.C., but one Frank Brown. Little did he know what he was getting himself into.

BROWN: "It was just one of the many games in which the Islanders would find a way to win, find a way to show how much character they had, how any team that wanted to learn how to win had to look at the example the Islanders set during that amazing period of time. This was a team that refused to lose. They held themselves to impossibly high standards and routinely exceeded them. Their dynasty was long over by then, but its descendants still carried that remarkable DNA.

"They were down 3-1 in this particular series and clawed back to force Game 7.

"The best part of (that) game day was getting to the rink hours early, before the doors were open to the fans and usually before the arena lights were turned up to game-brightness. I grabbed a cup of black coffee, headed down to ice-level and stared at the ice. Even if the lights were up at game power, what mattered to me was that the arena was empty and the ice was fresh, mesmerizing. A sacred place. I didn't need to stand there long to be filled with the power of the special moment I stole for myself before every game.

"Every other second of the entire day was devoted to thinking about what I had to be ready to write, to making sure I was prepared for anything that could happen, to having focus as clear and as cold as the frigid chill of the rink at ice-level. I was already fused to the information, the point-of-view, the attitude that was attached to the game; the necessary ritual was spiritually fusing myself to the ice so I would have a feel for it once the players were performing on it.

"There were occasions throughout my career when the coaches would allow me to put on my goalie equipment and face some shots at the end of morning skates. I loved doing that because it was cool and fun, of course, but I appreciated it because it helped me understand, on a profound level, the skills of the players I was describing. It helped my writing a lot. The players didn't mind because shooting at any goalie is better than shooting at an empty net or a sheet of canvas with holes in it at the corners. So that would 'get me in the game,' so to speak.

"During the game there would be lots of note-taking, lots more coffee. During the '70s, there were cigarettes, too. At the conclusion of the first and second periods, I would take out my computer, light up a Marlboro and start writing my 'running' story. After the game we would bolt to the dressing room, grab quotes from the players, listen to what the coach had to say and head back upstairs for more Marlboros, more coffee and the best sentences I could form.

"The Capital Centre in Landover, Md., was remote – far from the airport, far from downtown D.C. It had a black ceiling. And the press box was in the corner in the equivalent of the last few rows of seats. There was precious little light. At that time, computers were not very advanced; few of the computers reporters used were backlit. Surely mine wasn't. So it was difficult to see what I was typing. Tough to see whatever notes I was taking. It just wasn't a rink where it was 'fun' to work. Games there were to be endured, rather than enjoyed.

"The Capitals had some office space at Capital Center, and the office space was at the opposite end of the rink from the Caps' dressing room. So, often I would be typing my story or column, would look up for whatever reason and I always would pause to watch Caps GM David Poile and Caps Coach Bryan Murray walk through the empty stands toward their offices.

"They started at the near end of the rink, to my left, and would leave through an exit at the center of the far end, to my extreme right. The Capitals endured a lot of disappointment in the 1980's and a lot of it was inflicted by the Islanders or the Rangers. Many, many times, it looked as though Poile and Murray were not so much walking as trudging, bearing the weight of the world on their shoulders – a slow, sad walk in this dark building out in the middle of nowhere."

With the Hockey World watching, the Islanders and Capitals once again did battle as Game 7 got underway; neither team knowing what the outcome would be or how they would get there, each hoping they would be the last one standing.

The Capitals got off to a fast start, peppering Isles goalie Kelly Hrudey with shot after shot, but the 26-year-old from Edmonton, Alberta was a wall; stonewalling the Caps barrage with save after save. And it wasn't until the 19:12 mark of the first period that the Caps managed to break through, as Mike Gartner breached Hrudey's defenses to put Washington up 1-0 in the "do-or-die" game.

Normally, a goal that late in a period is a tough pill to swallow for the team that gave it up. But these were the Islanders, a proud group who had faced adversity before, even thriving on it. So it came as no surprise when 11:35 into the second period, Pat Flatley tied the game for the Isles by putting the puck past Caps goalie Bob Mason.

However, the tie didn't last long as Grant Martin put the Capitals back in front at the 18:45 mark of the second period. And while it was yet another late period goal surrendered by the Islanders, there wasn't much -- if any -- panic in them as both teams were sending an extraordinary amount of shots at the goaltenders. Surely another puck or two would find its way into the back of the nets before the game was through?

But as the third period got underway it seemed less and less likely that the Isles would be able to break through Mason's defenses again, that is, until Cup-stalwart Bryan Trottier revived a little of the Isles dynasty magic to tie the game at 2 with just 5:23 to go in regulation time.

BROWN: "They got a somewhat flukish goal from Bryan Trottier in the third period to tie the game to force overtime."

The Islanders had saved their season, but could they finish the job?

Overtime games are nothing out of the ordinary in hockey, be it in the regular-season or the playoffs. In fact, they are a fairly regular occurrence. But neither team managed to break through for a goal in the first overtime, so the game was headed to double-overtime.

BROWN: "(Al) Arbour was the Coach Emeritus, now a Vice President of the team. (Darcy) Regier was the Director of Hockey Administration. When the game had begun, they had sat with Bill Torrey, but Torrey had an overtime superstition: He would go down to ice level, find a place to stand by himself in one of the corners, and stay there until the game was decided."

Well, for Torrey's sake, he was certainly hoping the Isles would pull this thing off in the second overtime period. After all, it can get a little lonely standing there by yourself for so long.

However, even though the shots came coming, from both teams, nobody managed to score a goal and now this game -- this "winner-take-all" Game 7 -- was headed to a third overtime period. You may as well just call it "Game 8" at that point.

In fact, by the time the second overtime period had ended it was no longer Saturday night, rather, it was now Sunday morning, Easter Sunday to be exact.

But before we continue with the on-ice action -- or inaction -- let's check back in with Frank Brown, who along with the rest of the media, was watching the game from the press box and worrying about deadlines that were being messed up by the length of the game.

BROWN: "I did my best not to have personal feelings during the game, there was too much else going on. The simplest question was whether the Islanders – without Potvin, who was hurt; without Bossy, who was hurt -- were going to revisit their championship legacy or whether the Capitals were, at last, going to take that next step. It was all about the story lines."

So, while Brown and his colleagues worried about what their editors would say regarding them missing their deadlines, the Islanders and Capitals continued to wage war on the ice and growing ever more fatigued as the game pushed forward. And I do mean pushed, as neither team had much energy left in the tank.

After all, that's what happens when, after seven grueling games and three overtime periods and counting, you somehow find yourself rewriting the NHL's record books. And as the third overtime period came to a close the question became, "will this game ever end?"

For historical perspective, once the third overtime came and went without a victor, this was now the seventh-longest game in NHL history. (It has since been pushed further down the list, but let's stay in 1987 for now).

No NHL playoff game had gone to a fourth overtime since the Montreal Canadians beat the Detroit Red Wings on March 27, 1951. That's a whopping 36-years since the last quadruple-overtime playoff game!

So, the shots kept coming, from both teams, but could a winner be decided before this game had a chance to catch the Red Wings and the Montreal Maroons for the longest game ever? Which, by the way, was back in March of 1936 and had gone deep into a sixth-overtime period before ending in a Detroit victory.

Surely the players didn't want to play for THAT LONG. And the writers most certainly didn't want any part of that, even though, with their deadlines now since missed, they may as well have been fans at that point. In fact, one un-named writer evidently said, "let them play all night." Or perhaps he meant morning?

Nevertheless, this game was clearly in rarified company.

Could a hero emerge in the fourth-overtime? The Islanders definitely wanted one. And with 8:47 gone by they FINALLY got one.

BROWN: "In the fourth overtime, just short of 2 o'clock Easter morning, they got that turnaround goal from Pat LaFontaine to win. Again. Islander-style.

"I remember Caps goalie Bob Mason hearing the noise of the puck off the back of the net, looking around, realizing LaFontaine's shot had gone in – that an end had come to the game and the series and the Capitals' season – and then sinking to one knee. He seemed so tired, numb. Not so much defeated as deflated. I remember Rod Langway simply leaning forward, his stick across his knees, looking down at the ice. Stunned. I remember generalized Islanders bedlam on the ice and, in the front of the press box – several rows in front of me – Al Arbour and Darcy Regier throwing their arms around each other in one of the great hugs of hockey history."

And what of Bill Torrey, who had been standing all by his lonesome at ice-level since the beginning of the first overtime?

BROWN: "He was standing in the corner for a very, very long time. Arbour and Regier stayed in their positions in the press box and Torrey stayed in the corner, so he had no one to hug when LaFontaine's shot went in. Arbour and Regier leaped to their feet, hugged as though their lives depended on it – and setting loose great gusts of joy toward that ugly black ceiling."

And not to be forgotten was the fact that Kelly Hrudey had been just as much the hero as LaFontaine, as Hrudey made an all-time record 73-saves.

So, the game was finally over, but Frank Brown and company still had plenty of work to do.

BROWN: "(At that point) instinct takes over – who do I need to interview? What questions do I need to ask? What scene do I need to capture? In a game like that, the second the puck goes in, either you start typing or you bolt for the dressing room. In that instance, my recollection is that I bolted for the dressing room. The last deadline had long since passed; we all had written 'switch' leads – one for a 3-2 Islanders win, one for a 3-2 Islanders loss, one for an 'Islanders move on to face Philly after a fourth-overtime victory,' one for 'the Islanders' fight falls short in four-OT epic.' The desk would put in the name of the goal scorer, if possible. Really, this moment was more about gathering quotes and color for the Monday paper; we were long out of time on the Sunday edition.

"Somebody else was writing the main lead, which handled the Islanders and their reaction. I was helping out with the Capitals' side of things, and the Capitals' dressing room was an absolutely miserable place that night – more correctly, that Easter morning. Mike Ridley was on the bench when LaFontaine's shot caromed off something and got past Bob Mason. Ridley said, 'We heard the clank of the post, and then it was like you lost all the air out of your lungs.'

"The Capitals were good, just not good enough yet. Not ready to win, not ferocious enough. This was their fourth playoff loss in five April meetings with the Islanders. To that point, the Capitals never had won a game in which they faced elimination – regardless of the opponent.

"'The first time they beat us, I said it was a learning experience,' the Capitals' Mike Gartner said. 'The second time they beat us, I said it was a learning experience. Now, I really don't see anything else they can teach us . . . Maybe they can teach us how to win.'

"The post-game quotes were amazing after that game. Gartner's was one of the best, with Ridley's a runner-up. But in my view, the gold medal quote after that game came from the Capitals' PR guy, Lou Corletto. Lou was a great guy, a total pro in an unwinnable situation. His team had just lost to the Islanders – again. They had faced the cameras and the notepads and the tape recorders with glum stoicism – again.

"The fact was, all of us were LONG past our final deadlines -- the game had ended just before 2 a.m. – and there were no TV stations still on the air. Lou knew it had been painful enough for his players to lose and it was time for recovery to begin. He looked at his watch and raised his voice so any remaining media could hear. In an admonishing tone, he said, 'Folks, I'm closing this room at 3 a.m.'
I had never heard that said before; haven't heard it since."

A PICTURE IS WORTH 1,000 WORDS

BROWN: "They won the Stanley Cup in Vancouver in 1982, completing a sweep with a 3-1 victory at Pacific Coliseum. It was the year Roger Neilson rallied the Canucks and their fans by grabbing a towel, grabbing a stick, putting the towel on the stick and waving it at the referee in mock surrender.

"Being with a newspaper based in the Eastern Time zone, games in the Pacific west were hell with deadlines. Mike Bossy scored twice in the game, had some great things to say in memory of his father, Borden.

"I wrote the main lead, did a sidebar on Bossy and his Dad and then raced outside the rink in the hope I could get a cab to the airport in time to catch the team charter back to the Island. In those years, reporters travelled with the team; it wasn't a big deal.

"Of course, winning the Stanley Cup IS a big deal. Flying home promptly from Vancouver after winning the Stanley Cup is a big deal. I was sure they wouldn't hold the plane for me. As I worried about what I would do if I missed the flight, I remember waiting for the cab and looking across the street at the huge white flag flying from the pole on the Pacific Coliseum roof. There were spotlights on the flag, lighting it brightly against a clear, dark Vancouver night, the Canucks' final act of defiance.

"And I remember somehow getting to the airport, racing up the stairs to the plane and charging through the still-open front door. The entire team was on the plane. The Cup, of course, was on the plane. Either Bill Torrey or Al Arbour glared at me and said something like, 'About bleeping time, Frank' though their smiles made it clear they didn't really mind holding the plane for a reporter – even if it was the plane back to New York, carrying the Stanley Cup and the first American-based team to win it three years in succession."

5 BRENDAN BURKE (MSG NETWORK)
WELCOME BACK TO NASSAU COLISEUM!
(@NASSAU COLISEUM)
DECEMBER 1, 2018
NYI 3, CBJ 2

BACKGROUND

It's never easy for fans to accept change. And one-thing fans love to hold on to are the broadcasters who call their favorite team's games.

For Islanders fans, this is something they haven't had much experience with, as the likes of Jiggs McDonald and then Howie Rose, held down the Isles play-by-play duties for the better part of four-decades.

But eventually change did come for as the 2015-16 season came to a close; it became apparent that a new voice would be coming to the booth at the start of the following season. The question was, who would it be and, more importantly, would the Islanders fans accept the new guy as one of their own?

Well, the answer to the first part of the question is Brendan Burke, who, after nearly a decade in the AHL, finally got the call-up to the NHL. As for the second part of the question, I believe it is safe to say that Isles fans took to Burke almost immediately.

And now, in his fourth-season as the Islanders television play-by-play man, Burke is as beloved as any announcer in the NHL.

So, for those fans who don't know Burke's full-story, here it is; from his lips to your eyes and ears.

BURKE: "It started with my father, who is a sports writer and has been for my entire life. So, I grew up around the media side of sports; mostly around baseball as a young kid as my dad was the

Yankees beat writer for a few years when I was young. I would travel around with him every summer and get some unique experiences.

"I was actually born in Milwaukee, Wisconsin and I lived there until I was almost six. So, playing hockey and ice-skating is just part of the culture out there, from a young age. I was on the ice at 3-years-old and was playing hockey even before I moved out of Wisconsin.

"Hockey was just part of my life and I played it my whole life. I played travel hockey. I played high school hockey. I played club hockey in college. Hockey was my sport that I played and had a passion for, since the time I was little. I followed hockey, but I played hockey more than I followed the National Hockey League. With my father being a sports writer, I never really developed an affinity for any specific team.

"We just enjoyed watching games, watching sports. Whatever the best game that was on, if it was a Devils game, if it was a Rangers game, it was an Islanders game, or a national game, whatever the most compelling matchup that was on, that's what we'd watch. And so I never really grew up rooting for a team. I didn't really have any jerseys or posters on my wall.

"I just grew up appreciating the sport of hockey and sports in general. I guess that's a unique aspect of growing up, loving a sport, but not really loving a team or a player.

"One of my unique experiences with my dad led me to the radio broadcast booth for the Yankees with John Sterling and Michael Kay in it. I got to sit in there and see what they did and when I realized they got paid for doing that, that was when I decided that's what I wanted to do. I spent pretty much my whole life gearing up towards that. I went to Ithaca College and majored in journalism and spent all my free time at the radio and television stations there.

"Eventually, when I got out of school -- I graduated from Ithaca College in the spring of 2006 -- I got two jobs: one working in Minor League Baseball and one working in Minor League Hockey.

"I started, my first job out of school, that spring with the Batavia Muckdogs of the New York Penn League. I spent one-season there. That fall, in October of 2006, I got a job with the Wheeling Nailers of the ECHL. I did that for two-years, from 2006-07, through the 2007-08 season. I was bouncing back and forth with baseball the next two summers. I worked in the South Atlantic League for the Lakewood BlueClaws. That was starting in the spring of 2007 and then I also did the spring, into fall, of the 2008 season.

"So, I did all that for a few years until I wound up in the American Hockey League with the Peoria Rivermen. I started in Peoria with the Rivermen of the American Hockey League in the fall of October

2008 and I did that until the spring of 2013. Then, when the team moved, I got a new job, also in the AHL, in Utica, New York, with the Utica Comets. I moved there in July and the season started in the fall of 2013. I spent three-years there and ultimately got the Islanders job in the summer of 2016. It's been a long, winding road to get me here."

Of course, it wasn't just Burke's work experiences that helped shape him into the broadcaster he is today. Along with guidance from his father, he also had a proclivity for listening to other broadcasters so he could see what styles worked and how to shape his own on-air personality.

BURKE: "In terms of people who I looked up to in the broadcasting world, I grew up in Northern Jersey, right outside New York City, which was the perfect spot because I got to see all three New York area teams.

"I had 'Doc' (Emrick) on the Devils, Sam (Rosen) on the Rangers and I had Howie (Rose) on the Islanders. So I got to hear them on a regular basis. I think Gary Thorne was probably the prevailing national voice when I was a young kid, but then as I got older, I really made it a point to watch and listen to as many broadcasters as I could.

"One of the first things I did after college was get a satellite radio subscription where I could tune into broadcasters from all over the country. And so, I made it a point to hear as many as I could and that was kind of how I approached studying to become a broadcaster. I was just trying to absorb as much as I possibly could along the way.

"And it's something that I still do now."

While Burke indeed drew -- and continues to draw -- inspiration from his fellow broadcasters, one stands out above the rest. And that is his relationship with Howie Rose, who was instrumental in Burke's development.

BURKE: "When I was in college, or just out of college, my dad was covering the Mets. And so, through him, I developed somewhat of a relationship with Howie (Rose), in terms of, from time-to-time I would send him my broadcasting clips and get critiques and advice from him throughout the years. He was always very encouraging to me, even as a young kid out of school working in the lower levels of the minor leagues.

"And then, as I progressed in my career, he became a great advocate for me. Actually, a few years before I got the Islanders job, he would actually call other NHL teams when there were jobs open, on my behalf, to vouch for me along the way. He was somebody who was in my corner before the Islanders opportunity ever even came up.

"So, when the Islanders job came up, I obviously reached out to him and he kind of kept me calm and reassured me that my stuff was good enough and it'll take care of itself. He kind of helped me along there and I'm sure putting in a good word for me.

"But, throughout the process, he was great and to have him as somebody who I could call, text or email with any questions, was fantastic, because a lot of times broadcasters walk into a job where, with the guy walking out, it either doesn't end on good terms or whatever the situation is. They're not exactly the most helpful people to the person coming in to fill their shoes.

"So, I had the exact opposite with that. I had complete access to Howie, who was always there if I needed him. And obviously to have him be familiar with me and comfortable with me as the guy taking over, I think, was huge for me and was huge for my acceptance with Islanders fans, because I had him in my corner from Day One."

MOST UNFORGETTABLE ISLANDERS GAME

When the 2015-16 season began it was sort of like a soft reset for the Islanders franchise. They had just moved to Brooklyn from Uniondale, from Nassau Coliseum to Barclays Center and it was a chance for a new group of fans to be indoctrinated in "The Islanders Way."

Now, that's not to say the Islanders were leaving their old fans behind, it's just that their fans who lived out on Long Island were a bit resistant to changing their ways. They were used to driving to The Coliseum, tailgating in the parking lot and then taking a short drive home after games. Now, if they wanted to see the Islanders play, more likely than not, they had to take the Long Island Railroad. There were no more parking lot tailgates. No more short drives home after the games.

It was a new world, one in which things seemed very different, even if the players on the ice were still essentially the same as they had been during the 2014-15 season.

Oh and there was one more big difference, longtime broadcaster Howie Rose was no longer doing the play-by-play. In his place was a young, up-and-coming broadcaster by the name of Brendan Burke, who Rose himself had endorsed for the job. So, there was a new arena AND a new voice doing games for Islanders fans to get used to.

And as history will now show, only 50 percent of those changes did the Isles fans take to. They loved almost right out of the gate. Sadly, the same cannot be said for Barclays Center as their home arena. And after the initial buzz died down, Islanders fans made it known that they did not like the team's new home.

The ice was bad. The sight lines were awful. The scoreboard was off center. Those are just a few of the many complaints Islanders fans had about Barclays, not that there was much, if anything they could do about it. After all, the Islanders were locked into an ironclad lease, one that ensured they would call Barclays home for many, many years. Or so we all thought.

As it turns out, there were backroom discussions going on between Isles ownership, Barclays ownership and several other parties. And while some rumors were leaked to the public, only those in the know actually know what was being said.

So, in December 2017, when the Islanders and New York State Governor, Andrew Cuomo, announced the team had submitted a proposal to build a brand new arena in Belmont Park, the fan base rejoiced. Yes, the new arena wasn't scheduled to open until the 2021-22 season, but it almost didn't matter; the Islanders were essentially going back home, to an area where the majority of its fans lived.

And, in all the excitement, the team also announced that it had reached an agreement to play some of its home games during the intervening seasons at...you guessed it, Nassau Coliseum! The Isles were coming back home! All that remained was to pick the date. And that came soon afterwards, as the team announced it would make its glorious return to The Coliseum on Saturday December 1, 2018 against the Columbus Blue Jackets.

For the fans it was a dream come true. For the players it was a welcome return, even though, due to the team's youth, many had never played a game at The Coliseum. And for Play-by-Play man Brendan Burke; it was the missing piece in an otherwise stellar start to his career.

BURKE: "My first game at The Coliseum was the Islanders first game back at The Coliseum after their hiatus on December 1, 2018. I had never called a game in that building and for me, as an Islanders broadcaster, it always felt like something was missing, that I just didn't have the full Islanders experience, because I was hired in the era that was exclusively in Brooklyn. So, I was missing that Coliseum piece.

"To be able to come back to The Coliseum and experience what everybody had told me and all these stories that I had heard and what it's like to be in that building and the energy in the building was off the charts that night.

"It was interesting, because, I think, the story going into the game was obviously not about the Islanders vs. the Columbus Blue

Jackets. That was almost a secondary storyline to coming back to the building.

"Again, I wasn't there at the last game they played in before that and I wasn't really there for any of their games prior to that. I wasn't even alive for the Stanley Cups in that building. So, for me, it was just a lot of making sure that I had a good handle on the history and the significance of the building meant to the franchise, because as an outsider, as somebody who hadn't lived through that, that was something I knew was important for that moment, but something I didn't have naturally.

"So, I spent a lot of time going through old articles and I read a lot of the stuff that was written when the Islanders left The Coliseum initially with the expectation that they were never coming back. There was a lot of good history in those pieces and a lot about the greatest moments and all those different things that I tried to get a handle on. But that was more so in the days and weeks leading up to that game as opposed to actually the day of the game.

"The only thing really different on the day of the game was I wrote out the open to the broadcast, which I don't typically do. But for me it just felt like that moment deserved a little more than anything casually said to open the broadcast because it was such an important moment to the people who were watching. So, I took a few extra moments and scripted out something that I wanted to say at the top of the show.

"They even made a commercial out of the open that I said, 'The Coliseum is as it should be with the motions high and the ceilings low.' I just wanted to capture what it meant for the fan base to see the Islanders take that ice again.

"Now, the Coliseum is only one bowl, so there's no upper level and lower level. It's just kind of one bowl around and then the press box is kind of hanging from the roof a little bit. So we're (the media are) completely removed from where the fans are. But it's such a small building and such an intimate environment.

"They don't make buildings like that anymore, because they just don't function. When they built that building, the whole purpose was to give everybody a great sight line and it turned into a very unique building as everybody replaced their buildings, which were built in the '70s, and the Islanders hung onto theirs.

"It really was kind of like a time machine of going back into the glory days of the Islanders, because you don't get buildings like that anymore. It wouldn't matter if you were in the front row, in the last row, in the press box or in the parking lot; you were going to feel the emotion and the noise in the building that night.

"The Islanders fell down in that game 2-0. It took them awhile to get going.

"But once that first goal went in, Anders Lee scored a goal that actually needed video review to confirm that it was in fact a goal, that place erupted. And then it erupted again when they announced that the goal would stand. Also, Anthony Beauvillier scored a goal not too long after that and that place went absolutely bananas.

"I think that you knew they couldn't lose that game. That was the feeling going in, because it was a playoff atmosphere in a game that was played on December 1st. It was a Saturday night, but I mean it was a different environment than what you get in December no matter what. They fell behind 2-0. They gave up two quick goals in the second period early. And then you started to wonder, could they pull this off?

"Then, as soon as Anders Lee got that goal, you're like, all right, they're in business and the place is going nuts. And, hopefully, they can ride that momentum and they did. Beauvillier scored the goal two or three minutes after that before the end of the second period, so it was tied going into the third.

"Then it was, 'who's gonna flinch first?' And it was Casey Cizikas who scored. I remember the call because Butch (Goring) was talking during the play, because Ryan Pulock had come in down the wall and was looking for a pass or it looked like he was looking for a pass and he had a great chance to shoot the puck. And he didn't shoot it.

"He took it around the net and literally, when he didn't shoot it, Butch goes, 'I don't know why he didn't shoot that puck.' And before I could say anything, they made a pass to Cizikas and they scored. So, my goal call was, 'that's why!' Because he had already scored by the time I could get it out. And at that point it was just pandemonium in the building.

"I don't recall ever thinking that they were going to lose that game once they got the lead and sure enough, no one scored the rest of the game. It was a 3-2 final.

"(The funny thing is) I'm not sure, if you asked people on way out the door, if they could name the three Islanders goal scorers that they could do it, because it was just all about the moment of the game, the fact that they won it and the fact that they were home more than about the X's and O's and who scored to win the game and things like that. It certainly was a fun night to be in the building."

A PICTURE IS WORTH 1,000 WORDS

THE PLAYOFFS RETURN TO NASSAU! (@NASSAU COLISEUM)

APRIL 10, 2019
NYI 4, PIT 3 (OT)

BURKE: "Personally, it was exciting to call my first Islanders playoff game and something felt right about the fact that it was at The Coliseum. I think from the team perspective, it was more about the fact that, yes, it was The Coliseum, but they had home-ice in the first round of the playoffs. It was a season that started where nobody thought they had a chance at making the playoffs. All the talk was about John Tavares leaving during the off-season.

"So, to be able to put together the season that they had and get into the playoffs and then to get home-ice advantage in the first-round of the playoffs, that was a remarkable accomplishment. I mean, it was the first time in 30-years they had home-ice in the first-round of the playoffs. So it meant something that it was at The Coliseum, but it really meant something that it was a home game for them and kind of spoke to the season that they had.

"But, still then, I think what adds to the significance of that Game 1 win was, still no one was taking them seriously. Everybody had them pegged as underdogs, even though they were the home team in the first-round of the playoffs.

"They were taking on the Pittsburgh Penguins, who just have that winning pedigree and everybody expected them to win. And nobody believed that what the Islanders did during the regular-season was, I guess, real.

"They just thought they were winning with goaltending and some lucky shooting percentages and just kind of sneaking by. Really, nobody would validate the season that they had and they had to do it themselves by sweeping the Penguins in the first-round.

"That game went to overtime. If they lose that game, it's a very different series. But they won that game and they wound up sweeping the Penguins. It all started with that first game at The Coliseum.

"The play, it didn't take long. It wasn't even five-minutes into overtime that Josh Bailey scored the winner. It was a missed shot by the Penguins, that created a two-on-one with (Anthony) Beauvillier and (Mathew) Barzal. Barzal carried it in and seemingly had all day. Everybody expected him to pass and he didn't. But he waited everybody out to get a great opportunity and he went to the backhand and he hit the post. And in that moment he hit the post and the puck was still there.

"Josh Bailey, who was trailing the play was just charging up and I think he scored before anybody even realized he was there, or who it

41

was when he scored. And he put it in from a tough angle. It just kind of happened, almost in slow motion.

"It's one of my favorite calls because, when it ended, there's only so much you can say, right? And on television I have the luxury of not having to over describe it. It just is what it is. So I let the pictures tell the story. All I had to say was Josh Bailey, because everybody knows that there was a goal. So I said, 'Josh Bailey...Game 1 to the Island.'

"And it was not rehearsed. It was not planned. It was something that I've never said before in my life. But for some reason, in that moment, it felt like the game was won by more than just the guys on the ice, because it was back at The Coliseum and because there was so much energy in that building, that it felt bigger than just Josh Bailey or just the 18 guys on the ice.

"I don't know where it came from, maybe it was completely organic, but I think it fit the moment perfectly. Our director, Joel Mandelbaum, again, this is obviously not rehearsed, but he had the shot of (Robin) Lehner, 200-feet away from the celebration, sticking his arms in the air and it was just a perfect shot for that call.

"It just kind of worked. It's something that obviously I didn't necessarily appreciate or even understand at the time, but being able to watch it back and hearing everybody's reaction to it; it's certainly a, uh, a special call for me and I think for a lot of fans."

6 PAT CALABRIA (NEWSDAY)
"TONELLI TO NYSTROM...HE SCORES! BOB NYSTROM SCORES THE GOAL! THE ISLANDERS WIN THE STANLEY CUP!"
(@NASSAU COLISEUM)
MAY 24, 1980
NYI 5, PHI 4 (OT)

BACKGROUND

From an early age we all want to know what our destiny is. But rarely does destiny reveal itself to you, rather you have to find it on your own by carving out your own path in life. However, there are those rare few who just seem to know exactly what their future holds from their earliest conscious moments.

Sometimes your upbringing can dictate what your future holds. And sometimes you have to go out and make your own future.

But in the case of former-*Newsday* sports writer Pat Calabria, it's most definitely the former rather than the latter, that helped to make him into one of the top sports journalists of his time.

CALABRIA: "I always loved sports and my dad certainly introduced me to sports. I remember watching football games on a black and white Admiral TV when I was young. I remember very vividly watching the Ice Bowl between the Cowboys and the Packers in the minus-11 degree temperature in Green Bay.

"Growing up, I was a big baseball fan and still am. But like every other kid my age in New York, in the 1960s, my hero was Mickey Mantle and still is. I have a Mickey Mantle t-shirt, a Mickey Mantle bobble head and a Mickey Mantle card. I loved baseball. I played baseball in high school and played a little bit of basketball. I was late to come to hockey, although I followed the Rangers when I was young;

because that was the only team you could follow. The Islanders didn't exist yet. The Devils certainly didn't exist.

"I also always loved to write. I just did. It was something that came naturally to me. It's not something I had to work at. I feel, more than me choosing it, I was just blessed with it. And I don't mean that to sound immodest. It just came to me naturally and I was good at it. And since I loved sports, it was a natural marriage.

"For me, it really wasn't a choice to get into sports journalism. I have loved journalism since I was a child and my first paying job was when I was a high school junior, I think and I would cover my high school games for the local paper in Bethpage, Long Island. I was paid $16 a month. I would submit a story every week. I remember my dad driving me to the newspaper office on a Sunday night so I could drop off my typed up copy. I just loved writing. I always loved sports and participated in sports. So it was a great marriage. It's all I really ever wanted to do as an adolescent and a college student.

"I ended up going to Hofstra University where I majored in English. And I was Sports Editor of the student newspaper and later Editor-In-Chief of the student newspaper.

"I was hired as a college student helping out in the sports department when I was 19. I would take high school basketball box scores over the phone and cover high school basketball games. Then, in my senior year of college -- I graduated in '73 -- a job opened up and they offered it to me. It was covering high schools as a full-time staff member. So, my last semester of college, I went to class from 8am-3pm and then did my *Newsday* shift covering high school games from 4pm until whenever I finished.

"(And shortly thereafter), the Islanders captured my imagination, as well as the imaginations of a lot of people, in 1975 when they upset the Rangers in the first-round. They were down 3-0 to the Penguins in the Quarter-Finals and came back to win. They were down 3-0 to the Flyers in the Semi-finals and came back to tie. And by that time I was at *Newsday*.

"Right after that season -- the '74-'75 season -- I was asked if I would want to cover the Islanders and, of course, I jumped at the chance. I covered them from the '75-'76 season through the '83-'84 season when the Edmonton Oilers beat them in the Stanley Cup Final after they had won four straight Stanley Cups. And then I continued to help out on the beat afterwards. I was there for the Easter Epic in '87. But as the beat guy, I was there from '75-'76 through '83-'84."

MOST UNFORGETTABLE ISLANDERS GAME

When the Islanders entered the NHL in 1972, nobody could have imagined the level of success the team would reach within its first decade of play. Not that it was easy getting there though. From 1972-1974 the Islanders were perennial cellar-dwellers. But that all changed in 1975 as the team qualified for the playoffs for the first time in franchise history.

They upset the Rangers in an instant-classic series. They came back from down 3-0 to force and win Game 7 against the Penguins in the next round. They even went down 3-0 in the Conference Final to Philadelphia before storming back to force another Game 7 before ultimately succumbing to the Flyers. That playoff season put the Islanders on the map. And they continued to ascend to the top of the NHL every year as they again made playoff runs in 1976, 1977, 1978 and 1979.

By 1980 they were a battle-tested group that was one big win away from finally getting over the hump and calling itself champions. Once again they qualified for the playoffs in 1980 and this time, things were going to be different. First they knocked off the Los Angeles Kings three-games-to-one. Then it was on to the Quarter-Finals where they knocked off the Boston Bruins four-games-to-one. A Semi-Finals date with the Buffalo Sabres followed and this time the Islanders won the series by a four-games-to-two ledger.

Finally, it was on to the Stanley Cup Final for the first time in franchise history and their opponent was the Philadelphia Flyers. Would this match-up end the same way as it did in 1975? Or was it time for a new ending to the story? *Newsday's* Pat Calabria was there to witness the climatic series.

CALABRIA: "If you remember, the Islanders had a couple of years of disappointments. They were upset in '78, in the Quarter-Finals by the Toronto Maple Leafs. They were upset in '79, after they had led the league in points by the Rangers in the Semi-Finals.

"When you're covering a series like that, at least for me, my stomach churned a little. It was almost as if I was competing. I wanted to write the best stories. I wanted to have the best lead and wanted to have the best angles. I wanted to find out things nobody else was finding out. That's just the competitive nature of it.

"I remember very, very vividly, John Tonelli being pulled down around the neck in overtime. It was weird to call an overtime penalty and that was in Game 1. But it was clearly a penalty; the stick was wrapped around his neck. And I just remember Denis Potvin just walking into a shot, a one-timer to win the game.

"In Game 2 the Islanders came out flying in the first period early in the game. I really thought there was a possibility they were going to leave Philadelphia with a 2-0 lead. And, of course, the game changed very quickly and they lost something like 8-3, if I recall correctly. They went back to The Island for Game 3 and they won to go up 2-1.

"Now you start thinking, if they can win the next game at home, they'll be up 3-1 in the series; which is exactly what happened.

"Then they went back to Philly and they lost Game 5, 6-3. And remember the Islanders in '78, had 'choked.' In '79, they had 'choked' And now, the theme of some of the stories was, 'are they going to choke again?' Which was kind of silly, because they were up 3-2 going home and who wouldn't have bought that? You would have signed up for that.

"And I remember Garry Howatt saying, 'if somebody brings up the word choke, I'm going to choke him,' so they went back to The Island up 3-2 (in the series)."

Game 6 was played on the afternoon of May 24, 1980 at Nassau Coliseum. Could the Islanders close out the series and forever shed themselves of the "chokers" label that was beginning to follow them?

CALABRIA: "I don't think there's any question. If you asked the Islanders to this day, they'll tell you they did not want to go to Philadelphia and have to win a Game 7 in The Spectrum, which was just a crazy place. They were a confident group for sure. But certainly they did not relish the idea of potentially going back to The Spectrum for Game 7."

That was the backdrop for Game 6 and although the players tried to keep that out of their minds, it was an omnipresent warning that they really needed to finish the job in Game 6.

Of course, things didn't exactly start off smoothly for the Islanders as Flyers forward Reggie Leach opened the scoring at 7:21 of the first period with a power-play goal. Just like that, the Islanders' momentum was halted. Halted, but not extinguished.

Four-minutes and thirty-five seconds later, Denis Potvin netted a power-play tally of his own to tie the game and ease an early concern that may have been percolating through the Islanders bench or through the minds of the Islanders fans.

Potvin's goal was the spark the Isles needed to get things going and they made good use of it as they scored roughly two-minutes later to take a 2-1 lead. And the goal-scorer was Duane Sutter. Of course, his goal didn't come without a little bit of controversy.

CALABRIA: "Yes, one of the goals should have been called for offside, no question about that. I guess it was Duane Sutter who scored and the puck had been back-passed and drifted just beyond the blue line and they wound up scoring."

Thankfully for the Islanders technology wasn't anywhere near what it is today or that goal would likely have been disallowed.

And shortly after Sutter's goal, the Flyers' Brian Propp negated the damage by tying the game with a goal of his own to send the game into the first intermission tied at 2.

After the intermission the Islanders looked to regain control of the game, which they did, courtesy of two-goals scored roughly 12-minutes apart; one each from Mike Bossy (on the power-play) and Bob Nystrom. And so, the Islanders carried a 4-2 lead into the third period, with eyes on finally clinching the Stanley Cup.

CALABRIA: "I always maintained that if the Islanders weren't up 4-2, if they were up 3-2, they would have played differently in the third period, because they sat on that two-goal lead. Al Arbour was a great coach. A great defensive coach and a great guy. If they were up 3-2, I don't think they would have sat on that lead. At 4-2 they sat on the lead and, of course, the Flyers tied it.

"They were going to overtime.

"And it was sort of poetic justice that Lorne Henning, who was an original Islander and had been great in the playoffs that season, began the play. With Wayne Merrick hurt, Lorne Henning filled in for him late in the game and in overtime. Lorne got the puck along the right boards, passed it to Tonelli who crisscrossed with Nystrom. It was a play they had practiced like 9,000,000 times and Nystrom backhanded the puck past Pete Peeters in one motion and then threw his hands up in the air. Bob Dailey, who Nystrom had gotten past, I remember him sagging his head and it was pandemonium.

"I know there's some gossip out there that the winning-goal was offside. I've looked at the goal 100 times. It wasn't offside. Did the Flyers have a complaint about one of the other goals? Yes they did. But again, the game was 4-4 in overtime and both teams had an equal chance to win the game."

Just like that, the Islanders were Stanley Cup Champions!

But Calabria's tale doesn't end there.

CALABRIA: "I remember there were couples embracing and kissing and fans going crazy. I remember the locker room was bedlam. The wives were in the locker room. There was a whole bunch of media, of course. Guys were drinking from The Cup. And I remember asking Denis Potvin, who was the captain, 'how heavy is that Cup?' And he said, 'not so heavy I couldn't carry it.'

"I remember speaking with Lorne Henning, Lorne and I were very close. And he was saying that he was thinking of Dave Lewis, because he thought Dave should've been there. He had been an Islander since '73.

"I remember Wayne Merrick calling up a boyhood friend of his from Sarnia, Ontario, who he'd grown up with. I remember John Tonelli talking about what it was like to hold the Stanley Cup and when he was a boy, playing hockey in the living room and using an ashtray that he would hold over his head, like he won the Stanley Cup.

"It wasn't just about the game, but also about what happened afterwards. They won in '80, when you might've been able to argue that if they had disappointed again in '80, they might have really changed the team. But they won in '80 and continued to win. And so, that game kicked off the dynasty and kicked off the Islanders really being ambassadors for Long Island.

"Not only was the game exciting and momentous in Islanders history, but it kicked off a very momentous week. I mean, after the game, I remember being in a bar/restaurant (most of the players would go to a place called Dr. Generosity's in East Meadow, Long Island, five-minutes from The Coliseum. And so that's where I wound up) that the Islanders frequented. The roads were closed off and I knew the owner as well as I did the Islanders players and people were there until 4 o'clock in the morning.

"I remember Bobby Nystrom coming in the door about 1 or 2 o'clock in the morning and he was wearing a t-shirt that said, 'I'm proud to be an Islander,' and the place just exploded with cheers. Then there was the parade down Hempstead Turnpike. There was the passing around of the Stanley Cup and I actually convinced the PR Director of the Islanders, a fellow named Jimmy Higgins to let me have The Cup for a night and I threw a party for my neighborhood. I actually have a photo of my daughter, who's now a mom, and she was an infant at the time, sitting in the Stanley Cup.

"When The Cup got passed around to the players, as it traditionally does, I remember Clark Gillies telling me he let his German Shepherd, Hombre, eat out of The Cup. And I said, 'Clark, how could you let Hombre eat out of The Cup?' And he said, 'why not? He's a good dog.'

"I had great relationships with the Islanders. People who were around the team will tell you that was one of the best teams ever to cover. There wasn't any mistrust of the media. They were very accessible. The culture of the franchise was that the players should treat the media with respect. I became lifelong friends with lots of them. I'm still friends with many of the guys from those teams. It was a different time back then. I had players to my house for Thanksgiving. I double-dated with players. I just really treasure those memories."

A PICTURE IS WORTH 1,000 WORDS

CALABRIA: "I think it would be a picture I actually have; of me, Dave Lewis, Mike Kaszycki, Bobby Bourne and I think Pat Price may be in that photo too. It's at a place in Atlanta called Dante's and somebody took a picture of us. We had spent the night drinking at the bar after the game and it showed the kind of comradery between a writer and players that doesn't exist today. It just doesn't. If people want to say I was, 'too close to the team.' Okay, I was too close to the team. Guess what? I got a lot of stories nobody else did.

"It reminds me of the good times I had covering that team. I had a ball covering that team. I really did. They were a fun bunch to cover. I was young. I just ate and breathed hockey. I remember doing it during the playoffs. You'd cover the game and then I'd go back home or go back to a press center in a hotel if it was out of town and watch the game all over again. And I'd look for things I'd missed during the game. I remember listening to other games.

"I remember listening to overtime games between St. Louis and Chicago on the radio. I'd pick up KMOX on radio and just listen to those games. I'd talk to the Scouts. I went on a two-week scouting trip with Jimmy Devellano, the Islanders chief scout, one time. I spent so much time in hockey. I could map out my schedule for the whole year. 'Oh, there's a game. I'll be at practice. They'll have that Sunday off.' I could map out my schedule for the whole year."

7 HAWLEY CHESTER III (ISLANDERS PR)
PR DIRECTOR ALMOST SUITS UP FOR GAME AS PLAYER BUT
JUST MISSES OUT (@METROPOLITAN SPORTS CENTER)
MARCH 11, 1973
NYI 1, MNS 2

BACKGROUND

When the Islanders first came into the NHL they were nothing but a small operation trying to find its footing. But some very important and select individuals saw to it that the franchise was able to survive some early turmoil and eventually turn itself into an NHL-powerhouse.

Among the individuals who ran the off-ice operations, owner Roy Boe and G.M. Bill Torrey were the main masterminds at work. And after Boe and Torrey got things started, they soon brought in others to help as the team's first season drew nearer.

One of the people they brought in was a man by the name of Hawley Chester III, who has worked at the NHL office for a few years and who both Boe and Torrey knew at least somewhat well.

And being that this was and is a professional sports franchise, it was important to bring in somebody who could manage the public relations/communications end of things, as that is a crucial job for every professional team in the world; especially for a brand new one. Thus Chester III was brought in to make sure that the team had that department covered.

For Chester III, it was a continuation of a dream come true. He always wanted to work in professional hockey. And now, not only was he in professional hockey, but he was in on the ground floor of a brand new team; something that doesn't exactly happen every day.

So, let's learn a little but about who Chester III was and how he came to be in such an important position.

CHESTER III: "It's actually a pretty interesting story. I'm from a small town in Connecticut -- Greenwich, Connecticut -- right on the border of New York State. It was a wonderful place to grow up. I played hockey there. I was captain of my high school hockey team. Hockey was my passion from the time I was four or five-years-old. I started a little late, which was too bad.

"I was the lone person in my family skating. But we had a pond with lights within about 50-yards of my house. So, I learned to skate by pushing a chair around. When I was probably six or seven-years-old, we would play hockey from November to March. In those days, it was still cold enough in March, and the pond was fairly shallow, so it froze quickly and it would stay frozen throughout the entire winter. I would play all-day and night long with the lights on. I'd be playing until my mom would ring the bell at 11 o'clock at night and I would literally walk home in five minutes.

"Then, when I was at Denver University, we won two consecutive NCAA championships, my first and second years there. We had been third and fourth in the collegiate ranks in the NCAA tournament. So, I had four-straight years of NCAA championship hockey, of which I only played as a freshman at D.U. But then, I was involved with the team every day from that point on. I went to practice with them. I did stats. I did TV. I did radio. I did all the media things. And I basically was part of the team, the off-ice team if you will, for four-years at Denver University.

"That was the reason I went to Denver University, because of their hockey program. I knew I would be hard-pressed to play, as there was only one other Yank (Yankee) on the team, a guy by the name of Craig Patrick. And it was hard to qualify him as a Yank because he had played for the Montreal Junior Canadians.

"Anyway, one of my dearest friends and oldest friends is a guy by the name of Jeffrey Jennings. We were from the same hometown. Our fathers knew each other in college and before. Our mothers knew each other. And his father was the President of the New York Rangers. When I graduated in 1969 from Denver University, Jeffrey had been working for my father in the insurance business since the previous year, because he graduated a year ahead of me. So, I got a call that August, in 1969, wanting to know if I'd be interested in working for the National Hockey League office?

"Well, quite frankly, I was on my way to Law School, having been accepted to D.U. Law School. I was packing up the rest of my things in Connecticut to head back to Denver (when I got the call). And there was only one job (I would give up Law School for). I literally hung up the telephone after he called on that August day and I appeared at their front door and said, 'if there's an opportunity like this, of course I would give up going to Law School to go work at the National Hockey League.' It was my dream job.

"The only thing I had ever wanted to do was to work in professional hockey and I certainly wasn't going to play it, so I had to work in it. And here was my opportunity. That September I started to work at the National Hockey League Services Office in New York City. The NHL had just two offices, Montreal and New York and the Vice President of the NHL was a guy by the name of Don Ruck.

"I went to work as his assistant in September of 1969 and I was there for three-years in the office with him. It was basically he and I and three girls who ran the NHL's U.S. office: the television, the marketing, etc. All of the sort of domestic business attributes were run out of the NHL New York office. The League, the personnel and the administration of the players was run by Clarence Campbell out of the Montreal office.

"We had the two offices. We were the business headquarters, if you will and they were the administrative headquarters. So I worked for Don Ruck and Clarence Campbell for three-years and ironically, I think it was in November of 1971, I was at an NHL Board of Governors meeting and I believe it was at the Holiday Inn at JFK. It was not exactly a pretty place. In the summertime I guess it was nice, but it was where we held the Board of Governors meeting that created the Atlanta franchise and the New York Islanders franchise.

"I am probably one of the few people still alive who was at that Board of Governors meeting. And I was outside the door, guarding that door, along with our head of security for the NHL, when the two franchises were granted. I was probably the first person outside of the Board of Governors to find out that Long Island and Atlanta had been granted NHL franchises. And that's how I met the owner (of the Islanders), Roy Boe.

"He was somebody who I had known very well and he had been hoping to get the franchise. And he had spoken to me and said, 'if he got the franchise. If the NHL granted the franchise, would I be interested in being part of it?'

"Of course, having been in The League office, you always had half of the teams happy and half of the teams unhappy. When you're in the office, you don't hear from the happy teams much. But you hear from the unhappy teams all the time. It was a difficult job, because you're always balancing, trying to keep everybody as satisfied as possible or as happy as possible. And that's challenging. It's a challenging role. I did it,

I loved it and I enjoyed it. But I was ready to go pick a side and be on one side or the other."

And that's exactly what Chester did, as Bill Torrey, after conferring with Boe early in 1972, made the call to Chester to hire him as the Islanders' first VP of Public Relations. It was a post that Chester held for almost 10-years and during his time with the Islanders the team experienced many ups and downs, but through it all, he never stopped giving his absolute max effort as he tried to help the fledgling franchise grow.

MOST UNFORGETTABLE ISLANDERS GAME

If history teaches us anything, it's that first-year NHL teams -- with the exception of the Vegas Golden Knights -- usually don't perform all that well. Prior to Vegas' introduction to The League in the 2017-18 season, the rules for building an expansion team were very different and not at all friendly to the new franchises.

So, that's the situation the Islanders found themselves in when they joined the NHL for the 1972-73 season. Now, you can expect certain things to go wrong, like losing a lot of games or perhaps having behind-the-scenes issues as the team tries to navigate its' way through the NHL season.

However, one thing that is not expected to go wrong is having too few players for a given game.

And yet, that's precisely the situation the Islanders found themselves in on March 11, 1973, when they faced off against the Minnesota North Stars, in Minnesota, for the eighth-to-last game of what had been a highly disappointing first season.

CHESTER III: "It's the one (game) I regret the most. Near the end of our first season, we were playing in Minnesota and we had some injuries. We didn't have any players to call up, so we went to the game in Minnesota with only like 14 or 15 skaters. And unbeknownst to me, (Bill) Torrey and (Head) Coach Earl Ingarfield said they were gonna dress me, but they didn't tell me that."

Yes, you read that right. The New York Islanders were so short-handed and desperate for a healthy, warm-body that they were preparing to have their PR Director dress for the game as a player. Talk about a sticky situation.

CHESTER III: "I got to the arena that evening about an hour before the game and they said, 'you've got to get dressed.' Unfortunately, I had just had my pre-game meal before I walked over there, because I knew I was going to be in there for four or five hours and I hadn't eaten all day. So I'd had a fairly big meal at 5 o'clock. I did not feel like I wanted to jump in and go skating. So, when they said, 'get dressed,' I was like, 'Oh no, come on, you're kidding.' They said, 'Oh no, we're not kidding. You've got to get dressed.' And I said, 'no.'

"And I basically, at the last second said, 'no, I can't do it. I don't have my skates here or my stuff.' They said, 'we'll get you skates and whatever (you need).' Because I hadn't gotten there early enough to stretch or do anything to get ready to get dressed, I gave up. I said, 'no, I can't do this. I've gotta work upstairs in the press box.'"

Things could not have looked much worse for the visitors and the game hadn't even begun. If they were scrambling this badly before the game, you could only imagine what was going to unfold once the action got underway.

Well, for those predicting doom and gloom, the Isles actually jumped out to a lead, as captain Ed Westfall potted his 14th goal of the year at the 13:29 mark of the first period to give the Islanders a 1-0 lead.

So far so good for the undermanned Long Islanders. And so far, nothing to worry about for Hawley Chester III, who sat, watching from his perch in the press box.

Then again, maybe I've spoken too soon, because the North Stars were sending a bevy of shots towards Isles goalie, Gerry Desjardins. And while Desjardins was doing everything possible to hold onto the lead, it was a moment of frustration for him that caused Chester III to look down at the ice with regret.

CHESTER III: "Well, lo and behold, in the second period, Gerry Desjardins was playing goal and he got a major penalty, a five-minute major penalty and they had to take somebody and have them serve the penalty for him. Of course, had I dressed, I would have been the person who would have served the penalty. When the penalty ended after five-minutes, I would have had to literally go on the ice and skate across to the bench and be replaced by one of the Islanders players.

"So, I was sitting in the press box thinking, 'my God, that would have been me serving the penalty.'"

Granted, the Isles killed off the penalty without much fuss and he certainly wouldn't have had any real action, but it was a light-hearted moment that made Chester III look back with guilt at his pre-game decision.

And, of course, the Islanders still had the rest of the game to play. But what happened next wasn't pretty for Chester III or the players down on the ice.

With the Isles clinging to their 1-0 lead it looked like they might actually get out of dodge with a rare win. But it was not to be as Danny

Grant scored twice for the North Stars in the final three-and-a-half-minutes of the third to steal a win from the Islanders and send the visitors home with yet another defeat.

CHESTER III: "Later (after the game) they (Torrey and Ingarfield) were joking about it because I would have been the first PR Director to have actually dressed and played, because I would've had to cross the ice to go sit on the bench. At that point, they were activating me as a player and they were going to sign me to a contract. I wouldn't have gotten any money of course, but they would have had to notify the NHL that Hawley T. Chester III had dressed and was under contract for the New York Islanders.

"That's a moment that everyday in the mirror I shake my head and realize, because I had one big meal at the wrong time, I basically missed my opportunity to be the first PR Director to have actually played in a game. That's one that I will never, ever forget. It would have been a unique moment."

And if you think Chester III had regrets about the game, how do you think Desjardins felt? He made 44-saves, played his tail off and was still saddled with a loss.

History may not look back at this game as anything other than an Islanders loss, but it could have been so much more. And not a day goes by that Hawley Chester III doesn't think about his decision to have a large meal before the game.

So, there's a lesson to be learned from all this and that is, don't eat a lot before a game, because you never know what opportunities may come your way.

A PICTURE IS WORTH 1,000 WORDS

CHESTER III: "At The Nassau Coliseum, the locker rooms were in a hallway on the, I think it would be, the west side of the building.

"We came in on the west side, so the locker rooms for both teams were in that west corridor, I think it is. And I created a hospitality media room pressroom if you will. We would serve food or drinks or whatever and the media would meet in there before, during and after the game. We'd have guys who would file their copy.

"I know it's hard to believe, but guys carried typewriters around to games. They had to. You had to carry your typewriter and you literally wrote on the spot in the pressroom and then we would send the copy to the home and road newspapers.

"And down that hallway were two big garbage cans. I made my office at Nassau Coliseum at those two garbage cans. In those days I smoked fairly heavily, unfortunately. I was a heavy smoker of Marlboro Reds. I would be by those two garbage cans from say two-hours before the game, all the way through to the end of the game. I'd either be up in the press box or I'd be down there at those garbage cans.

"If anybody needed anything, they knew where to find me. Whether it was a media member or someone from the team, whether it was (Al) Arbour or the owners. I was close enough to either dressing room or the pressroom, so if there were ever an issue with anything, I would be there.

"So they jokingly called that my office at the Nassau Coliseum. The big garbage cans were my office and I was there for eight-years in that one spot. It was a concrete jungle. That's where I was happiest. It was a fairly unique office."

JOHN TAVARES SCORES NOT ONCE BUT TWICE, ENDING
ISLES DROUGHT
(@BARCLAYS CENTER)
APRIL 24, 2016
NYI 2, FLA 1 (2OT)

BACKGROUND

In some cases, the apple doesn't fall far from the tree. And it's really a terrific experience for all involved when a son -- or daughter -- manages to follow in their parent's footsteps in terms of crafting a professional career.

For current NHL.com writer, Brian Compton, it was the experiences he received early on, as a child going with his father to work, that helped lead him down the path towards becoming a well-respected NHL reporter.

From meeting Al Arbour as a toddler, to going around the Islanders dressing room after practices, Compton grew up with keen insights into the world of journalism and especially the Islanders.

But just because he grew up around the team, that doesn't mean he had an easy path getting there on his own once he grew up.

COMPTON: "Well, I'm kind of second generation following in my dad's footsteps. He used to take me to Islanders practices in the early-80s when they were the best thing going. I got to meet all the players, be around the locker room and meet Al Arbour.

"I knew even back then that I was probably never going to be a pro-athlete. I just didn't have it in my DNA. I just thought it was a really cool job. My dad would go on the road and always come back with something for me and my siblings, stuff like that and I just thought it was a really cool job.

"It took a lot of time to get to where I wanted to go. I went to King's College, which is in Wilkes-Barre, Pennsylvania and I graduated in 1999. Then I worked for *The Post* right out of school in 1999, for two-years and got laid off like everybody else does in this industry at some point or another. So then, I was a sports editor for the *Southampton Press* out East for about 11 months. And then I covered Minor League Hockey for six-years -- from '02-'07 -- which was a really cool experience.

"I made a lot of good contacts down there and met a lot of good people while covering guys who probably knew even then that they weren't going to ever play in the NHL. They were just really passionate about playing and were still following that dream, even if it was a pipe dream for a lot of them.

"Then I started freelancing for the NHL around that time; probably my last season or two that I was covering in Trenton I was doing a weekly ECHL update for the NHL. And it just led to the job back in New York, which was great for me because that's home. I was born and raised there obviously. So it's really worked out.

"It was mostly editing when I joined The League and then I got into the Islanders full-time around '09, probably around the time they drafted (John) Tavares. I think from that point on I've been focusing on them."

MOST UNFORGETTABLE ISLANDERS GAME

From 1980-1984, the Islanders won 19 consecutive playoff series. It is a feat that will likely never come close to being matched or bested. And from 1984 to 1993, the Islanders, while they won no Cups, still had some moderate playoff success.

So, for a team with such a rich playoff history, for them to go over two-decades without winning a single playoff series should have been unheard of, if not impossible. But that's exactly the position the Islanders found themselves in from 1993-2016. For you see, after ending the Penguins' bid for a third-straight Cup in 1993, the Isles did not win another playoff series until they faced the Panthers in the opening-round of the 2016 playoffs.

That's like an eternity, and then some, for Isles fans who grew up during the team's Cup-years. Now, that's not to say they didn't have chances to end the drought sooner, because they did. There was the tough seven-game loss to Toronto in 2002. There was the series against Pittsburgh in 2013. And there was also the series against Washington in

2015 that acted as a final sendoff of sorts for Nassau Coliseum; at least that's what the plan was at the time.

So, going into their first-round series against the Panthers in 2016, in their new Brooklyn digs, the Islanders and their fans had no reason to expect a turnaround in fortune was in-store. Although, the fans certainly hoped and prayed with all their might that 2016 was finally going to be their year.

The series started down in Florida with the teams splitting the opening two games; the Islanders won Game 1 by the score of 5-4.

And after losing Game 2, the Isles came back to Brooklyn and earned a hard-fought, overtime victory in Game 3 to take a 2-1 series lead.

Multiple sources will tell you that the team who wins Game 3 in a playoff series to take a 2-1 lead goes on to win the series more often than not. But these were the Islanders, a team who numbers alone never could define.

And then came Game 4, also in Brooklyn, which the Isles lost 2-1 and essentially turned the series into a best-two-out-of-three.

COMPTON: "I was traveling with them, because I always traveled with them in the playoffs. That's really the only time that I do travel with the team. So I was tired. It ended up ending in six, but it felt longer. I guess it was because Game 5 went to overtime and once you get to five, six and seven, it's pretty much every other night. And then it's different cities going back and forth.

"So there was some travel involved there and Game 5 was obviously very dramatic with (Thomas) Greiss stopping a penalty-shot in overtime. And then Alan Quine, who probably played five-games all season and was a spare part bouncing back and forth between the Islanders and Bridgeport, for him to get that goal in overtime, that was pretty cool."

With the Game 5 win behind them, the Islanders came home for Game 6 looking to put the series away. But to do so wouldn't be easy.

COMPTON: "That's the other thing about the series, they really weren't the better team five-on-five. I mean, Florida really outplayed them, for the entirety of the series.

"The thing I remember the most really was talking to Ray Ferraro in the morning (of Game 6), because he had played such a big role in that '93 team. I think he scored two or three overtime goals. He probably led the team in goals overall over the course of that playoff run they had.

"He was just saying how special it was that he was able to be in the building, should they win. How he was proud to be an Islander and all that good stuff. The players were pretty focused. They knew what they had in front of them. They knew how much pressure was on them to finally get the franchise over the hump after 23-years. And they had the character to deal with that pressure.

"Whether it was Tavares or Travis Hamonic and Matt Martin and Josh Bailey, they just had a lot, a lot of character in that room. And Doug Weight was an Assistant Coach who had a ton of character and was a great guy. Everybody knew what was on the line and they particularly knew that having a 3-2 series lead that they just had to get it done that night. They didn't want to go back to Florida for a possible Game 7.

"And then, the one caveat (for me) with the games in Brooklyn and not in Nassau County was you had to spend all day in Brooklyn. So it's a really long day. You're on the train at I guess 8:30 in the morning to go to the morning skate, because the Islanders would skate in Brooklyn on game days.

"Then, I had to cover the Panthers skate as well. So the day started at 8:30 (AM) and it wouldn't end until probably past midnight for me. So, the routine was basically, go to the morning skate, write a preview or a column, then there was a lot of sitting around for a couple hours waiting for the game to start. And then, I think I did the recap and a column that night. So it was probably a 15- or 16-hour day for sure."

With all the pressure on the Isles could they actually pull through; especially against a team that was outplaying them for much of the series?

COMPTON: "I guess what I really remember is sitting there with them losing for the most part of the game and getting out-played. I remember in Game 6 when they were down, just thinking, 'man, now they've got to go back to Florida and win another game.' This probably was really their big chance to get over the hump and win the series, because anything can happen in a Game 7. I know anything can happen in a Game 7, but they won Game 6 against the Caps the year before and then lost Game 7.

"I really thought they were going to lose that series because of the way Game 6 had been going."

Uh-oh, that's not exactly a good feeling to have. Would the Isles be able to right the ship before Florida sank them for good? To do so, they would need a hero. And lo-and-behold, they got one.

COMPTON: "John Tavares tied the game, I think in the last minute, with (Thomas) Greiss pulled. On the Tavares tying-goal, I think somebody had shot it from the point and (Roberto) Luongo thought he had it in the crease.

"But he just clearly lost sight of the puck. He thought that he had it and it was just sitting in the blue paint by itself and nobody really noticed it except Tavares and he just kind of pounced on it. You could see just the relief and the joy in his face. The crowd just went nuts. The place was shaking. I mean, it was really, really loud in there. And I think everybody knew, once he tied the game, that they were just going to find a way to win it in overtime.

"I think the players felt that way. I remember the fans, between the third period and the first overtime, it was like the old days at The Coliseum. They were just so thrilled to be in this position and with a chance to win the game in overtime and move on to the second-round."

But as everybody in attendance soon found out, one-overtime would not be enough to determine a winner, so, double-overtime was needed. And for the writers like Brian Compton, any potential winning goal would have to be seen on the TV set in the press room down below, rather than live from the press box.

COMPTON: "For the writers, it's so hard to get downstairs (at Barclays) after a game, unless you're already downstairs. If you try to get down there from section 212 when everybody's kind of leaving at the same time, it's really difficult.

"So all of us were in the press room watching on TV and there was probably a 5- to 10-second delay from the live action. We heard a woman scream, I don't know if it was an Usher or somebody out in the corridor, outside the press room.

"So, we knew something was coming. And then you just heard this roar.

"We looked up at the TV and we were able to see the goal unfold. Tavares got the puck in the right circle and he took a wrister that Luongo stopped. He got his own rebound and skated around the net and beat him to the far post on the wraparound to win it. I think my first words, honestly, were 'Holy Sh*t! They're finally going to the second-round of the playoffs.'

"I'm sure that's what Howie (Rose) wanted to say on the broadcast but he couldn't. I wish I could have been in my press seat to see it happen live. But I think we were still able to capture it. Whether it was that woman screaming and knowing that it was coming, maybe that helped. I don't know. But you could still tell how incredibly loud the building was even being down in the pressroom when he scored that goal.

"And that's what made what Tavares did so heroic. He tied that game late and then won the game in double-overtime. It really was the culmination of everything Islanders fans were expecting from John when they took him first overall in 2009.

"(When they won) I was so happy for the fans, because I knew firsthand what they had gone through with all the ownership changes and having to leave The Coliseum. And, at that point, we never thought that they were going back there.

"For the fans to finally see their team play beyond the first-round of the playoffs, which is absurd. I mean, you see the Bruins or the Blackhawks who, they do this year in and year out. It had been a long time to go without winning a playoff round. So, I think I was just happy for the fans.

"And I remember going into the room from the player's perspective, Travis Hamonic was actually shaking in his stall. I mean, he was just, you could tell for the guys who had been there for a while. I mean, Hamonic was drafted in '08, Tavares in '09, (Josh) Bailey in '08 and Frans Nielsen in '02, I was really happy for those guys who had been there when things were really, really bad.

"I mean that '08-'09 team, the year before they drafted Tavares and even the '09-'10 team. I mean those teams were so bad. So, to see them get over the hump and obviously it took longer than they would have expected because they had a few pretty good first-rounds before that.

"In '15 against the Caps, when they lost in Game 7 or the shortened season in '13 when they really went toe-to-toe with the Penguins, which was a lot of fun to watch. To see them finally get over the hump, that was just a really, really cool moment for the players and the fans.

"I also remember, vividly, Tavares, he's very robotic and he's very even keel in everything he says and does. But you could tell how excited he was in his stall. I don't know if he was shaking to the point that Travis was, but he had an extra pep in his voice so you could see how excited he was.

"They knew what was on the line and they knew how much pressure was on each and every one of them to get over the hump and win a playoff round. So, maybe it was because he was the one who scored those two-goals to get them there. Whatever it was, because really, at the end of the day, John Tavares and Thomas Greiss stole that series."

A PICTURE IS WORTH 1,000 WORDS

COMPTON: "I would have to say Game 3 of the 2013 first-round against the Penguins. During The Anthem I was just sitting, probably wasn't in the same seat my dad was in all those years ago, but I just thought it was really cool to be covering a playoff game in the same arena. I mean, it had the same feel, the same look; it was before they redid the building, so it was really the same.

"Everything was the same, certainly in the press box, it's probably the same chairs. I mean, those chairs are a billion years old. I was just really proud to be able to do that. It wasn't the Stanley Cup Final, that's still on the bucket list for me obviously, but to be in the same building where he covered a lot of those playoff games, during the greatest run by the franchise ever; I just thought that was a really cool moment for me and him."

9 ERIC COMPTON (NY DAILY NEWS)
FOUR-STRAIGHT CUPS IT IS! (@NASSAU COLISEUM)
MAY 17, 1983
NYI 4, EDM 2

BACKGROUND

It's not everyday that you get to start your career at the top. Normally it takes a long time to get to that particular point. But every now and again luck shines on you and you get to live out your dreams.

For Eric Compton, it wasn't a matter of "IF" he wanted to become a sports writer. Rather it was a question of, how long would it take?

Compton's lifelong passion for sports was a precursor for his eventual career; all he needed to do was take the necessary steps. And while some may argue that he never quite started at "Square One,' that's not really a fair criticism to make.

There's an old saying that chance favors the prepared mind. And in Compton's case, he was well prepared, regardless of nerves, to succeed when his opportunity came knocking.

That opportunity came in the form of a job with the *New York Daily News*, right out of college. And while he "skipped" the step of starting out at a smaller paper, it wasn't like he was given the most prestigious beat right away. Rather, he earned his assignments through sheer hard work. And in the long run, it paid off as he was assigned to cover the last true U.S. based hockey dynasty.

So, without further ado, here's how he got from Point A to Point B, C, D, etc.

COMPTON: "Well, I grew up just outside of New York City with my father, who was a huge sports fan. We'd go see baseball games. We'd go to see hockey games. I remember my first hockey game; he took me to see the Rangers, who were playing the Red Wings. And, I remember, on the way down, I said, 'who should I watch,' because I knew the Rangers weren't very good. And he said, 'keep an eye on number nine on Detroit. He's pretty good.' And it turned out it was Gordie Howe. So, I was always interested in sports.

"I just thought going to sports games was the greatest thing ever. And I remember thinking, 'how great would it be to actually go to a game and not pay, but have someone pay you to go to the game.' So, I got interested in journalism. I wrote for the high school newspaper and then went to Marquette University, got a journalism degree out there and came back.

"And it's kind of an unusual story because I started at the top. I started at the *New York Daily News*, whereas most people work their way up to the top. *The Daily News,* at the time, was the largest paper in the country. I'd gotten a job there during the summer while I was in college, so, when I got out of Marquette, I went back to *The Daily News*, started at the bottom and just worked my way up. I always wanted to write about sports, but I had to wait about five-years to get a promotion into the sports department. I started out doing just the scoreboard pages, compiling the agate, the standings, the horse racing and that kind of stuff.

"Then, after a couple of months, they kind of discovered that I could do more than just agate and decided to have me start covering games off TV from the sports department; like college basketball. Eventually, a job opened up on the desk and I became a copy editor, which lasted for only about three or four months. And then they decided to make me a writer.

"I started out doing college basketball and college football. I was the college guy at *The Daily News* for about two-years and then the Islanders beat opened up in January of '82. I was living on Long Island at the time and the Sports Editor called me and said, 'Mary Flannery, who's our writer is leaving. Would you like the Islanders beat?' I was kind of nervous about it, because you're watching sports all your life, but until you're covering it, you don't really understand what's going on.

"So, I was very nervous. I mean, who starts out their hockey career covering what was one of the greatest teams ever? So I was very nervous about taking the job, but I went in there and I was in over my head when I started. But it worked out and I covered them through the rest of that season when they won the Stanley Cup and the following season ('82-'83) when they won their fourth in a row.

"My first game was in January of '82 and it was a road game in either Minneapolis or St. Louis. It was a two-game trip. I got a lot of help from the other people on the beat, even though we were in competition.

The editors would always stress that you had to beat *The Post* on this story. You have to get something *Newsday* doesn't. It really wasn't like that with the writers though. We were all pretty close. I got a lot of help from Doug Gould, who was the Islanders beat writer for *The Post*. I got help from Tim Moriarty and Pat Calabria at *Newsday*.

"We were all friendly. The team used to take us out for dinner during the playoffs. I remember one night, in Quebec City, when God only knows what kind of bill we ran up. Mark Everson of *The Post* saw the wine list was all in French and he just decided to order bottles of wine. I don't know what Bill Torrey's reaction was when he saw the bill, but it was $700 or $800 for like 12 of us.

"So it wasn't the typical success story or the typical buildup to a career where you have to pay your dues at a lower level. I mean, I paid my dues, but it wasn't writing everyday at a smaller paper. I started at the top and then basically stayed there."

And while Compton, "stayed there," he was able to witness some magical moments for a team that was in the middle of one of the greatest runs in hockey history.

MOST UNFORGETTABLE ISLANDERS GAME

The 1982-83 season was a trying one for the Islanders. The mission was clear, win a fourth-straight Stanley Cup; something that only the Montreal Canadiens had ever done. But in order to get there, they had to go through a league that was forever improving. And as three-time defending champions, they had a target on their backs.

COMPTON: "The Islanders had gone through so much that season. They were shutout six-times, but they'd won three Cups in a row and the team just had this feeling that whenever they had to turn it on, they would be able to do it.

"And they did.

"Stan Fischler used to do a between period show and then he did a playoff preview show before the playoffs. And I remember sitting down with him and basically embarrassing myself because I said, 'I don't think this team could do it this year.' They didn't score a lot of goals in the regular season. They seemed to be coasting on several nights, just figuring, 'well, when the playoffs come, we'll be able to turn it on.' They didn't play very well in the playoffs in the first couple of rounds, they kind of struggled.

"And then all of a sudden they turned it on and when they got to the Edmonton series, you looked at Edmonton and saw the talent on that team and I remember talking to the other writers and you just said, 'this team is going to be great.'

"I mean you saw (Mark) Messier and you saw Paul Coffey and you saw (Wayne) Gretzky and you saw Jari Kurri and you saw the goaltending, which was underrated, because they were facing 40-shots a night and you just thought, 'this team is going to be the next dynasty.'

"You didn't have free agency then, so there was no real thought of teams breaking up, which really helped the Islanders, because if you'd had free agency when the Islanders were at their peak, the Rangers would have come and offered (Mike) Bossy or (Denis) Potvin or (Billy) Smith or (Bryan) Trottier millions of dollars; or hundreds of thousands of dollars.

"The Islanders never would have been able to stick together. But, when you got to that series against Edmonton, you just thought, 'wow, it's like the changing of the guard.' And everyone knew how good Edmonton was. They'd just blown through the playoffs in the first three rounds.

"Well, Game 1, Bossy had tonsillitis and he didn't play. We were in Edmonton and the Islanders got a late first period, early second period goal, it might've been (Wayne) Merrick or (Bob) Nystrom, I'm not sure. And they held on and won. They shutout Edmonton in Edmonton. And I remember looking at the other writers thinking, 'wow, this is amazing.' They just shutout a team that had scored 350, 400-goals.

"So, they got to Game 4 and it was just one of those nights where the Islanders got off to a great start. The crowd was just roaring, because if anybody had said before the series that the Islanders were going to sweep this team, you woulda 'thought they're nuts. They're absolutely crazy. There's no way they're gonna sweep Edmonton.' I mean, there was even thought that Edmonton might beat them. Even as young as Edmonton was, they had so much talent.

"Well, we got to Game 4 and the Islanders got three goals early and the crowd was rocking. The goals came really, really quickly. Trottier scored on a power-play like midway through the first period to open the scoring.

"Then, while the teams were still cheering that goal, Nystrom went into the corner and just stripped someone on Edmonton of the puck and sent it in front and (John) Tonelli stuffed it in. So they got two-goals in 43-seconds and then they scored less than a minute after that. Bossy scored on a pass from Trottier. So, it's 3-0 in a span of 97-seconds. They got three-goals and you thought, 'it's absolutely over. There was no way Edmonton was coming back.' It was just going to be a question of how big the lead was going to be.

"But, at the same time, at that point Edmonton had absolutely nothing to lose. I mean, you're down 3-0 (in the series); no one gives you a chance anyway, so they were playing loose, cocky and there was just this feeling that maybe the series wasn't over.

"Then, in the second period Edmonton scored two 'Edmonton goals.' I mean, I don't know if anybody else could've scored those goals. Gretzky got the puck behind the Islanders net and made a pass that probably only he could have made. I mean, he faked one way with the pass and went another and Kurri was standing in front and he slammed it home. I don't think Smith ever moved. I don't think Billy ever saw where the puck was. All of a sudden it was in the net.

"Edmonton was getting the better chances the whole second period. They had a power-play midway through the period where they had a couple of really good shots on net and Smith just stood on his head. And just as the period was about to end, you thought, 'it's 3-1, they can carry a 3-1 lead,' and then Messier scored on a shot from the circle with 21-seconds left in the period. All of a sudden, it was, 'wow, it's a 3-2 game.' It's a totally different game. Now Edmonton has momentum. Now it's anyone's game.

"And I remember talking to one of the Islanders early in the series. I think it was probably Bob Bourne and he said, 'you never want to play a Game 7, because even if you've got more talent, it's a bounce of a puck. It's the way the puck comes off the boards. It's one play. It's, you lose your edge and all of a sudden the puck is in the net.'

"So, I remember thinking about that, that night. I mean, the Islanders were up 3-0 on this team and you thought the game was basically over. And then Edmonton just dominated the second period. Now it was 3-2.

"The third period was one of those periods where you kind of had the feeling that if Edmonton scored again, you didn't know whether the Islanders could have gotten that fourth goal, because Edmonton had carried the action through the second period.

"Well, what happened was, Billy Smith faked getting hurt on a high stick. Just when it's a 3-2 game, he went down like he got shot and the referees called a penalty, even though there really wasn't one. It totally threw Edmonton off down the stretch.

"The Islanders had just gone off on a penalty and Edmonton was putting on pressure on the power-play. Glenn Anderson was in front of the net and he kind of raised his stick, but it was kind of held by an Islander. It was one of those things where they were just vying for the puck and Billy went down like he was shot.

"Obviously, today they would never even think of that as a penalty because they would have gone to replay and seen he didn't get touched. Billy wasn't touched and he went down. And not only did they call a penalty, they called a five-minute penalty and that killed off the Edmonton power-play, plus another three-and-a-half, almost four-minutes.

"It should not have been a five-minute penalty, but they called it. Would Edmonton have scored if they didn't call the penalty? You don't know. I mean, they would've been on a power-play. There was still 11-minutes to go when, so they would've been on a power-play and theoretically, with that kind of talent, they might have scored.

"I remember that one play because no one was really looking at them. You follow the puck so much that you didn't really see what was happening in front until after it had happened and you saw Smith, his head went back and then he went down. We all went, 'what happened on that?' We had replays in the box, but we all just looked at each other and said, 'he didn't get touched.'

"Billy was one of those guys where he didn't really talk about it afterwards. He didn't admit that it was a total flop. But I remember him saying, 'you gotta do what you gotta do.' It was just one of those moments where, do the ends justify the means?

"It didn't take away Edmonton's last chance, but it certainly hurt their chances, because by the time Anderson came out of the box, they only had a couple of minutes left.

"They pulled their goalie with about a minute-and-a half to go and the Islanders just managed to keep the puck away from Smith until Kenny Morrow got the puck, took a couple of strides towards center ice and just put a puck right in the center of the net.

"I mean, that's how perfect the shot was. He just slid it right along the ice and it just went right, straight into the net, so they won 4-2. I remember, when Morrow's shot went in the net there was this sign of relief, like, 'Oh my God, it's over.'

"The scene in the locker room afterwards was just unbelievable. I mean, I think it was, the team didn't know it was over, but in talking to them afterwards, all they talked about was how good it felt to beat a team they knew was going to be great. I mean they beat that Edmonton team that had something like six Hall of Famers on it.

"When they beat Edmonton in Game 4, it was unabashed joy. I mean, it was just players embracing each other and The Cup. And the look on Trottier's face when he hoisted that Cup and Denny Potvin's face and Mike Bossy's, I think that there was that feeling of relief, because I think in the players' minds, they knew that Edmonton was one day going to take over from them. At that point the Islanders weren't an old team at all, but they had played four-straight years of playoffs, which no other team had done.

"I mean, to play four-straight years in The Finals like that, starting that fifth year, they were up against teams who were so much fresher than they were and Edmonton was so much younger. So, that '83 Game 4, when that puck went into the empty net, The Coliseum just exploded.

"And the look on the players' faces when they did it, even though, by that time it was old hat because it'd been the fourth year and you don't get the same feeling that you got in the first year. It was just this utter fatigue. And they wanted to celebrate, but a lot of them were just so tired after the whole chase and everything. It was just phenomenal to see.

"I remember, the hard thing about working games at The Coliseum was going down the stairs since there was no elevator at the time, all 82 or 83 steps and then I had to climb back up the stairs to do my writing. And that night I only had like 20-minutes to do so because I had a midnight deadline; this, of course, after doing the interviews downstairs.

"I remember coming up those stairs and thinking to myself, 'that's the last time I'll have to do that this year.' That feeling of coming up the stairs for the last time, it kind of gave me the feeling like, 'okay, I can do this. I can get this story out.'"

A PICTURE IS WORTH 1,000 WORDS

COMPTON: "I think it would be in the 1982 playoffs against Pittsburgh. John Tonelli scored the winner and overtime and he jumped up in the air. They were down 3-1 with less than eight minutes to go in the third and we're sitting there in the press box and I remember Pat Calabria turning to me saying, 'it's over;' that The Cup run is over. They'd only won it twice at that point.

"I had to think it was over the way Pittsburgh had come back after getting blown out the first two games at The Coliseum and then beating us in Pittsburgh the next two. So, the Islanders were down 3-1 and Al Arbour switched his goalies just to gain some time. Back then there was a rule that if you changed your goalies, the backup goaltender had a couple of minutes to warm up; very much like a relief pitcher in baseball.

"So, Arbour used that to get his players more rest after they scored the second goal to make it 3-2; that way he could put his top-line on again. And then the Islanders tied it with about three or four minutes to go. The one scene I remember is Tonelli scoring in overtime and just jumping in the air. The look on his face and the look on (Bob) Nystrom's face and the other players on the ice was just very similar to when Nystrom scored The Cup-winner in 1980. It was very much the same kind of pure elation.

"They were down and got two-goals in the last five-and-a-half minutes. (Mike) McEwen scored on a power-play with five-and-a-half minutes to go and then Tonelli scored from right in front with about two-and-a-half minutes to go to tie it. And then Tonelli got the winner in overtime and again, it was him and Nystrom. There may have been better players, statistically, like (Mike) Bossy and (Denis) Potvin, but in terms of heart, John Tonelli and Bobby Nystrom were everything the Islanders were. And that vision of Tonelli jumping in the air after scoring in overtime, that is something I'll never forget.

"John Tonelli was not the most talented player in the league, but he had as much heart as anybody I've ever seen. When he scored that goal, we kind of jumped up in the press box because we said, 'wow, they won't have a scare like that again.' And they didn't the rest of the playoffs. I mean, once they won that series, they just coasted. But that one moment when he scored, that still sticks with me."

10 STAN FISCHLER (SPORTSCHANNEL)
LET THEM PLAY ALL NIGHT! THE EASTER EPIC
(@CAPITAL CENTER)
APRIL 18, 1987
NYI 3, WSH 2 (4OT)

BACKGROUND

"The Hockey Maven," Stan Fischler, is known across the NHL as one of the brightest minds in the game. And when the calendar flipped to 2020, he entered his eighth decade covering hockey, both as a writer and as a television analyst.

Stan Fischler has authored over a 100 books, most of them hockey related, and has earned numerous accolades during his time covering the New York Rangers, New York Islanders and of course, the New Jersey Devils. Oh, and let's not forget about his stint broadcasting games for the Hartford Whalers.

While "The Maven," hung up his microphone following the 2017-18 season, he still keeps himself active as a prominent hockey historian for the NHL's website, as well as for the Islanders' and Devils' websites; consistently creating various forms of material for fans to learn about the great game of hockey.

But before he became "The Hockey Maven," -- a nickname given to him by current Vancouver Canucks Head Coach, Travis Green, when Green was still an active player -- he was just another kid from Brooklyn, New York, who was fascinated by the game of hockey.

FISCHLER: "I went to my first game at The Garden in 1939, when I was seven and I instantly became enthralled with the game. But I was too young to go to the Rangers' games, so I went to the Rovers' games -- they had double headers on Sunday afternoons. The Rovers were really terrific. There were MET League games, which were local players. It was not limited by age and there were four teams: the Sands Point Tigers, Manhattan Arrows, The Jamaica Hawks and The Stock Exchange Brokers, who became The Brooklyn Torpedoes during World War II.

"There was a wonderful preliminary game at 1:30 and then at 3:30 the Rovers would play. The Rovers were the Rangers' farm team in the Eastern League. Just excellent hockey, exciting, I loved it. Rangers games at that time started at 8:30, so my parents wouldn't let me go because it was too late and I had school the next day. So I didn't go to a Rangers game until 1942.

"In '42, for my 10th birthday, my parents gave me a little Philco Radio, it was called the Transitone and a scrapbook with an Indian Head -- it had a three dimension Indian Head on it. Those were the catalysts for my love of hockey. With the radio, I was able to pick up Canadian games from Toronto, with Foster Hewitt announcing. He was very, very exciting, so I became a Leafs fan just by listening to him. To this day, there has not been an announcer to equal Foster Hewitt the way he called a game. There are a lot of wonderful announcers, but Foster was The Dean.

"With the scrapbook, I started to clip stories out of the papers, which, at that time, were just the New York papers. So in 1942, the clippings started. And this was all part of my hockey infatuation. I was an only child, so hockey was like my brother in a way. It gave me something to do. I still have every scrapbook, starting with 1942. It was a different type of hockey journalism. It wasn't as intense as it is now, but it was more fun.

"By the 1946-47 season, when I started High School, I was a crazy Leafs fan. Once, I was down at Times Square going to see a movie at The Paramount with my friend Howie Sparer and while I was waiting for him I was standing at 43rd between Broadway and 7th, where the old Times building was. At the bottom there was an out of town newspaper stand. It was a big deal; there were papers from all over the country and Canada.

"While I was waiting for Howie, I saw there was a newspaper called The Toronto Globe and Mail, it was only a quarter. I picked up the paper, turned to the sports section and saw all these hockey stories that weren't in the New York papers. Of course, the main stories were about The Leafs. I was amazed. It was like I was discovering gold.

"That night, I went home and opened up to the Editorial page and saw I could subscribe and it wasn't that much. So I subscribed and everyday, one day after it came out, I was getting it in my mailbox; I was only getting The Globe one day late. The stories and the writing were wonderful. I found one particular columnist named, Jim Coleman, who I emulated in my head, because I loved his style. I had all his columns in my scrapbooks. I had one scrapbook for every year and it was all Leafs. That was the year they won their first Cup out of three in a row (1946-47).

"By now, I was old enough to go to the Rangers games, which I did. My friend Jimmy and I became season ticket holders -- End Balcony section 333, row E, seats five and six. Just wonderful seats at The Old Garden, the End Balcony. Before that, when I was going to the Rovers' games, I would get a program and it had a lot of white space and on the roster page there was also a lot of white space. So, at the end of every game, I'd write stories on my own, which, in retrospect, was an indication that I liked to write.

"When my teams won it was a wonderful story. But when my teams lost, it was the referee's fault. I couldn't write hockey in High School, I did very little writing in High School. When I got to Brooklyn College in 1950, we didn't have a (hockey) team, but we did have a soccer team and I got to write about them. Soccer was very big and it was a great experience. That, plus one journalism course, taught by Phil Leddy -- no relation to Nick Leddy on the Islanders -- who was the professor had a profound influence on me.

"So, in 1951, the Leafs won their fourth Cup in five years. Bill Barilko scored the winning goal, he had been my hero. But then he disappeared in a plane crash -- him and another guy. They were heading to the fishing area in Northern Ontario when they disappeared. They didn't find them for 10 years.

"I remained a Leafs fan through the 1951-52 season, but by that time, Herb Goren had become the Rangers' press agent and he formed a Rangers' Fan Club. I went to the first meeting; they had a few players there. It was very exciting. And I said, 'wow, this is for me.' So, myself, along with two other guys -- Fred Meier, who I'm still in touch with (we played roller hockey together) and Jerry Weiss -- decided to put together a Fan Club paper -- The Rangers' Review.

"At that time, the PR guy, Herb Goren, who formed the Fan Club -- it wasn't fans who did it, it was the Rangers -- allowed us access to the players. The first guy we wanted to interview was Eddie Kullman and he was a good, tough, checking forward. A lot of the players, the day of the game, stayed at the old Belvedere Hotel, which was across the street from The Old Garden. So, me and Freddy went up, before Kullman took his pre-game nap and we interviewed him. He was wonderful. We couldn't believe it.

"Then, as the Fan Club grew, I stopped being a Leafs fan and I became a Rangers fan and I became the Vice President of the Fan Club. Gradually, with all the writing, I had access to all the players and The Garden; I was also going to all the Rovers' games. And I knew the guy who ran the Rovers. His name was Tommy Lockhart, who was also a business manager for the Rangers. So, one day, I went to Tommy and I suggested that I write a newsletter about the whole Eastern League. It was very important to me and it would cost them nothing. So he said do it and every week he'd distribute my stuff.

"So, when I graduated from Brooklyn College in 1954, that September, Herbie Goren offered me a job in publicity, as his assistant. It was like the old cliché, like dying and going to heaven."

And after getting a foothold in New York, Fischler quickly became a household name with his various columns on all things NHL. Eventually, Fischler transitioned to television -- while still keeping up his writing -- and was working Islanders games.

FISCHLER: "I was writing for the *New York Journal American*, covering the Rangers. And I was also writing books, so I was very busy on the writing side. I never expected to do anything in terms of television. But when the World Hockey Association came along, there was a team in Boston, the New England Whalers. And at that time, I was very critical of the Bruins. I was viewed as very anti-Bruin and I was very vocal about it on *WEEI* in Boston. My buddy, Eddie Andelman, who did the show, had a lot of connections and one of them was with Howard Baldwin, who was running the New England Whalers; playing at Boston Garden.

"Eddie called me up and said, 'how'd you like to do hockey?' I said, 'I'm not interested in television, I'm a writer, don't bother me.' He said, 'you could make some good money doing it.' So I said, 'give me an idea of what you call, good money.' What he told me was astounding, compared to print.

"So I said, 'it sounds like you're not going to be able to get that kind of money, you're just teasing me.' He said, 'well, I'll see about that.' He called me back the next day and said, 'I got exactly what I told you.' So I said, 'alright, I'm on.'

"That's how I started in television.

"The second year I was doing the Whalers, I got a call from Marty Glickman, who was the Dean of New York Sportscasters.

"Marty said he's friendly with a guy named Chuck Dolan. Nobody, not even me, knew who Chuck Dolan was then. And he said Chuck Dolan is going to be doing a telecast of an Islanders home game and how would I like to be the color commentator? I said, 'are you kidding?' Everybody wanted to be in the NHL. I did it with Spencer Ross, who did the play-by-play and that was the first year the Islanders made the playoffs; 1974-75.

"We jumped from the end of the season to the playoffs, with the first series being against the Rangers and the Islanders beat them two-games to one. Then we did the Penguins and the Islanders came back from being down three-games to zip to beat the Penguins in seven games. And then we played the Flyers. And we went down three-games to zip, tied it at three and then the Flyers beat us in Game 7. So, the Islanders had become a name and that's how I wound up doing the games.

"For most of the early years I was doing the color. And then, in 1979-80, Eddie Westfall, who was the captain, retired and they put him up in the booth with Jiggs (McDonald) and I did the between periods interviews. Essentially, I've been doing Islanders stuff ever since."

MOST UNFORGETTABLE ISLANDERS GAME

The 1987 playoffs were a chance for the Islanders to exact a measure of revenge against the team who dispatched them for Lord Stanley's Tournament the year prior, the Washington Capitals. But in order to do so, the Islanders would need to dig down deep and conjure up some of the same magic they so often displayed at the peak of their dynasty earlier in the decade.

First they had to overcome a 1-0 series deficit after losing the opening game 4-3. Then, after tying the series with a 3-1 Game 2 victory, the Isles went down three-games-to-one following consecutive defeats in Games 3 and 4; putting them on the precipice of back-to-back early playoff exits.

But if there was any team who could come back from such a deficit, it was the Islanders, who had made similar comebacks seem almost routine from 1975-1984. And so it began, as the Isles won Games 5 and 6 by a combined score of 9-6; thus forcing a Game 7 down in Landover, Maryland on Saturday night April 18, 1987.

At that point, the Patrick Division Semi-Finals winner was anyone's guess, but one person was cautiously optimistic and pessimistic, all at the same time. And that person was the Hockey Maven, Stan Fischler, who was also the Isles Studio Host for *SportsChannel*.

FISCHLER: "Washington was favored, it was their home game and I was always nervous about how the game was going to go. I thought the Islanders were going to lose because they were down and

Washington was a very good team. (Plus), being half-Hungarian, I'm generally a pessimist, so I always felt The Islanders were going to lose, that is, until they won."

But, if the Hockey Maven was nervous, he didn't show it early on. That came later.

FISCHLER: "I always wanted to get there earlier than anybody else and get the feel of the arena. And I always did the interviews with the coaches and players, visiting and so on, particularly in the playoffs. And, of course, after a game I was always pretty exhausted (that night especially)."

However, as the game went along, Fischler's nerves grew. (I can only imagine how the players must have felt). And after being down 1-0 at the end of the first period, the Isles tied the game midway through the second, courtesy of a goal by Pat Flatley. But even that tie didn't last long for the Caps' Grant Martin restored Washington's lead late in the period and the home team held onto its lead until there was just under five-and-a-half minutes remaining in the third period. And then a hero emerged for the Islanders.

FISCHLER: "People don't know this, but just before Bryan Trottier scored the tying-goal against Bob Mason, Mason's skate broke. Bryan was beating a goalie with a broken skate. Of course, nobody knew about it at the time, it's only recently that Mason talked about it. And, of course, the fact was that it became a tied game."

And it stayed a tied game through the end of regulation, thus forcing overtime.

FISCHLER: "The goaltending was spectacular. It was Kelly Hrudy against Bob Mason. Hrudey said it was the best game ever played. When you say, 'spectacular goaltending,' right from the get go, you wondered how long it could go. And Hrudey made something like 70-plus saves in that game.

"And, the other thing that was very interesting was that Andy Van Hellemond was the veteran referee and for the most part he let the guys play the game."

He certainly did, "let them play." In fact, they played their way from one overtime, to two, to three, to four before a victor could be declared.

FISCHLER: "By the third-overtime, you could tackle somebody and it wasn't going to be a penalty. And there was a lot of that. It was, in the end, one of the (most) outstanding goaltending (battles), for both sides, of all-time. But, clearly, Hrudey made many more saves than Bobby Mason.

"Anyway, I was (working) alone, working in this little studio and I nearly got killed by the way, I think it was during the second-overtime. I was watching the game and the only guy in the studio with me was John McComb, who was my Stage Manager. And I was so into it that I was making saves for (Kelly) Hrudey, doing this and that.

"On one very close call, I fell back in the chair out of excitement and I fell so far back that I was going to hit my head on the concrete floor. But, (thankfully), John McComb dove and grabbed my head just before I killed myself. That was unforgettable. If I had killed myself, it would have been forgettable.

"(Aside from my near accident) I had a major problem, apart from being nervous, which I always was at the games; more so back then. My job was to get interviews and I actually got Mike Bossy twice, because we couldn't find people to interview. There was competition from the networks. So, that was the biggest challenge. And, of course, it wasn't easy. Bossy was hurt, that's why I was able to get him twice. And I also got Denny Potvin.

"I have written about every one of the longest games, including the longest one, which was in 1936 and last six-overtimes. And a part of me was hoping that it would go to six and never end. Of course, working on the Islanders side, I wanted the Islanders to win."

That's a lot to digest for just one man as he's hoping for and trying to will the Islanders to victory. Luck for him, the fourth-overtime brought about the end of the game, in a somewhat awkward fashion.

FISCHLER: "It was a play that wasn't supposed to be. I remember it vividly because Gord Dineen was one of the young defensemen and he wasn't that good, good kid though. And Gordy Dineen was at left defense and on that play, when the puck went behind the net, Gordy Dineen vacated his spot. I said, 'what the hell? Is this guy crazy?' He's supposed to stay back.

"Well, when he went behind the net, Patty LaFontaine came over the boards and immediately covered for him. And then, Dineen tried to stuff the puck on kind of a wraparound. It bounced off Rod Langway and it went skittering out to Pat LaFontaine. Patty said he'd never taken a shot like that before. He kind of spun around like a toy table hockey player. And Dale Henry, who was a fourth-liner on the Islanders, screened Bob Mason, as did Langway to a certain extent. And that's how it went in. That's billiards luck.

"I was delirious when LaFontaine scored. It was very hard to tell it was a goal right away because of the screen. Mason never even saw the puck. LaFontaine didn't even know it had gone in. He thought the, 'clang,' meant it had hit the post and gone into the corner. So, there was a very pregnant pause before we knew what it was all about.

"After Patty LaFontaine got the winning-goal I was able to get Patty (for an interview) because we had been pals. When they came off, they walked past our studio to get to the Islanders dressing room and we grabbed him before he even got to the dressing room. So, I had this fantastic interview before anybody else with one of my favorite guys.

"And after I did LaFontaine, then I had to do the room and obviously, it was a very joyous but very, very tired room. What made it even worse was that the bus took us to the charter and there was a tremendous lightning-thunderstorm, so the charter was delayed. Everybody was beat to hell hanging around waiting. We got back to New York and it was Easter Sunday. When I finally got into bed the phone rang and it was Bob Raissman of *The Daily News* wanting an interview with me about the whole thing.

"I wasn't going to say, 'no,' to Bob Raissman, so I did the interview and then I couldn't fall asleep. So, I got on my bike and I rode along Riverside Drive, along the river for about an hour-and-a-half trying to recall whether I was dreaming about that hockey game."

It wasn't a dream, but nice sentiment.

A PICTURE IS WORTH 1,000 WORDS

FISCHLER: "Bobby Nystrom's OT goal that won the first Cup was extraordinarily special, for a lot of reasons. The Isles had never won a Cup. They were leading Philly by two-goals going into the third period, everybody in the joint thought the thing was in the bag. And I kept saying, 'no, no, no, no, no.' Sure enough, right off the bat, the Flyers scored in the first minute-and-a-half or so. I think it was a defenseman who scored the goal. Anyway, two nobodies tied the game. The Flyers were all over Billy Smith. If it wasn't for Billy Smith being Billy Smith, the Flyers would have taken over the game. So it went into overtime.

"The ironic part of it was, that on that play, the center who started it normally would have been playing; that was Lorne Henning. He was replacing Wayne Merrick and he started to play by passing it to Johnny Tonelli, who was on his wrong wing. This was a play they normally would have done in practice and many times. But here they were doing it a** backwards. Tonelli was on his wrong wing. That's why the pass to Nystrom was not pure. But, Ny managed to get his stick on it. He didn't shoot it. He really deflected it. So, they wound up winning The Cup."

11 ALAN HAHN (NEWSDAY)
THE ISLANDERS STRIKE BACK IN GAME 6!
(@NASSAU COLISEUM)
APRIL 28, 2002
NYI 5, TOR 3

BACKGROUND

Long before Alan Hahn became one of the top basketball analysts and top radio voices around, he actually cut his teeth as a writer for *Newsday*. And no it wasn't basketball he was writing about, although that did come later.

In fact, it wasn't even pro sports he was writing about.

HAHN: "When I started out, believe it or not, I didn't even have a byline in the paper for the first couple of months.

"I would just take calls over the phone from coaches, high school coaches, who would give a score and you'd write these little blurbs, two, three lines at best; you didn't get any credit for it. I did that for a couple of months. And then, little by little, I'd get an assignment, mostly I did some high school games and then I moved over into doing a lot of local college stuff.

"That was the majority of my experience. There was a little bit here and there of, 'Hey, we need somebody at this Jets practice,' So we'd need somebody at whatever else was going on that I would have to cover. But it was very rare. I had no pro experience whatsoever. But, I proved myself as a writer who could cover things, get the story and write features. I think I proved my stuff, even though it wasn't big-time sports I was covering.

"I always say (to young people trying to get into the business), 'you don't come out of college and want to just dive into covering pro sports. It's not as easy as you think. If you can cover a high school game and make it sound good (that's good experience). My first byline was a badminton game in high school. If you could make high school badminton sound interesting, then obviously you get to the pros; you can do anything. So that's kind of how it went."

Granted, Hahn didn't always plan on becoming a writer or analyst. He was actually a collegiate athlete who was unfortunately struck by the injury bug before he could ever make it to the pros.

HAHN: "I played college basketball and I got injured while playing in college. So it was one of those things where if you can't play it (may as well cover it). I always liked coverage. I always liked sports talk radio. I always liked the different broadcasts that I would watch.

"I grew up listening to the Islanders on radio, believe it or not, because my family, we didn't really have a lot of cable channels back in those days. You had to pay for them, we didn't really have a lot of money and I grew up in a Rangers household, so they would pay for *MSG* but they wouldn't pay for *SportsChannel*. So, a lot of times I was in my room listening to the Islanders games during their Stanley Cup era on radio.

"And I was fascinated by the media coverage; the media part of the business. So, when I went to college, I sort of just thought, 'if I don't make it as an athlete, I want to at least be around sports in some way.' So I took journalism as a degree and when I got hurt, it became a reality where I said, 'okay, I really gotta get into this.'

"That's how I got a part-time job at *Newsday*, basically because they recognized my name because I was in the paper as an athlete. It wasn't for anything I had done, because I didn't really have a lot of experience. I didn't have an internship or anything. I had nothing. I just walked in the door basically and said, 'I have this journalism degree. I'd like to be a writer.' And I got a part-time job.

"It took me about five-years as a part-timer before I had a chance to really become a beat writer. And it so happened, the Islanders beat was open. They offered it to me in 1999 and not a lot of people wanted to cover the team back at that point because they really were a mess. The Spano thing had just happened. They had issues with the arena.

"No one really cared about them like they used to back in the old days. In the '80s and the early-90's the Islanders were a premier beat for *Newsday*. That was a big deal because it was our team. But by the late-

90's, nobody really wanted to deal with the headache of covering all the drama around it, on top of the fact that the team wasn't very good.

"But I jumped at it because it was my first chance and I said, 'I'll do it.' So that's how I got the job. Essentially it was offered to me before I was about to leave the paper and they said, 'no, no, no, we want you to do this.' And I said, 'Sure, I'm in.' So '99 was my first time ever on a pro beat and it was quite a time to jump in covering a team like that. (To be precise) Training Camp in September of '99, at Lake Placid was my first experience on that beat, covering the Islanders.

"In my first year on the Islanders beat I actually won what was at the time called, *The Newsday Publisher's Award*, which was given out to the best writer in each division (of the paper).

"I won it for sports that year, in my very first year, because again, there was so much going on with that team. It was a lot to do and I was on top of it."

MOST UNFORGETTABLE ISLANDERS GAME

The 2001-02 Islanders were a team looking for a change. First thing's first, at the end of the previous season, the Islanders decided to move on from Head Coach Lorne Henning, who had replaced Isles' icon, Butch Goring during the season. The team needed a new Head Coach for the '01-'02 campaign, so it decided to sign Peter Laviolette for the gig.

With a new Head Coach in place, the Isles also were on a mission to end the longest playoff drought in franchise history, having not been to the dance since being swept by the Rangers in the opening-round of the 1993-94 tournament. And as it turns out, Laviolette was the right man for the job as he guided the team to a 42-28-8-4 record and a second-place finish in the Atlantic Division.

With a playoff spot secured, the Isles turned their attention to their Quarter-Finals opponent, the Toronto Maple Leafs. Both teams deserved to be there, but only one could advance to the next round.

HAHN: "That series was less about the goals that were scored and more about the physicality.

"For the Islanders it was a good season. I think they missed the division by like a point or two. They got the Maple Leafs in the first-round and the Maple Leafs were a pretty good team. Then the Islanders went to Toronto and they looked over-matched in the first two games. They just didn't look like they were going to be competitive in the series. And I remember, Mike Milbury, who was the GM, between Games 2 and 3, one of the writers said to him, 'it's been a pretty good season. You've got to feel good about the season' and he was mad. He said, 'we're not doing any retrospectives here. We've got a series to win.'

"You could tell he was mad and he showed us this video that was about 10-minutes long of penalties that the Maple Leafs were getting away with; that there weren't any calls. And he must've used the F-bomb about 20 times while he showed us this video, of all these things that the Islanders weren't getting calls on and he got fined heavily for doing that. But it took all the pressure off his team. And so, going into Game 3, instead of writing about how the Islanders were over-matched, it was more like, they were mad about the fact that they thought the Maple Leafs we're getting away with stuff.

"So Game 3 happened and the Leafs had some issues. I think Pat Quinn made a couple of mistakes, they ended up winning that game and now they felt like they were back in the series.

"Game 4 obviously was a really exciting game. And then (Shawn) Bates got the penalty-shot goal and the Islanders won that game. And now you felt like, 'they're back in this thing.' So that was kind of the setup (for Game 6).

"That turned the series and then, obviously, Game 5, Kenny Jonsson got hit by Gary Roberts on a dirty hit. He got a concussion. And then, Michael Peca and the infamous hit by Darcy Tucker, behind the play, Peca blew out his ACL and he was their captain and their best penalty-killer. So the Islanders lost their best defenseman and their best two-way player in one game. They lost that game and they came home and you were thinking the series was over.

"But that Game 6, you could just feel it in the parking lot. The Islanders weren't ready to quit. It was a pretty wild night. It was the most incredible atmosphere I've ever experienced as far as covering a game at The Coliseum.

"They were down 3-2 in the series and you could just feel it in the building. There was just something special in that series. Obviously, in Game 4, there was the penalty-shot by Shawn Bates that everybody talks about from that series and the building shook when he scored. But, to me, Game 6, there was just something about it that you could feel before you walked in the building.

"I went to the morning skate, which was the thing you do because you got both teams. I remember I spent the whole day there. I didn't go home that day. I decided I was just going to stay there all day because it was that big of a game. So, the routine was essentially getting there in time for the Islanders skate; talking to Peter Laviolette. I'll never forget when I saw Steve Webb, who was one of their grinders, a tough guy fourth-line type who played a physical game and he hadn't gotten in the lineup yet. But, because of the injury to Peca, they needed to put another forward in the lineup.

"That morning, we got word that even, though they didn't make it official, it was like a hint, that Webb was probably gonna play. And if Webb was going to play, that meant they wanted to play tough. They wanted to add some toughness. And so, I saw Webb walking by, he was a great guy, and I remember saying to him, 'you're gonna go tonight?' He said, 'it sounds like it.' So I said, 'have fun.' And he went, 'you know, I will.' And he gave me this look like, 'you know what I'm about.'

"Also, Billy Smith, who was their Goaltending Coach at the time, his whole thing was that he didn't believe in the handshake after the game (when he was a player). He felt, 'why am I shaking hands with somebody I just beat? I just took away your chance to win and now I'm going to shake your hand?' He never believed in that.

"So, one of the writers said to him, 'Hey, if the Leafs win tonight and the series ends, do you think these guys should shake hands with them after what happened in Game 5?' And he went nuts. Again, this was between the morning skate and the game and we were at The Coliseum. He just said, 'no. Why should I shake hands with somebody who gave one of my players a concussion?' He was just so charged up about the physicality of the series.

"It was a real charged atmosphere. It was one of the most fun games I've ever covered as a sports writer. But as an Islanders beat (writer), it really stays with me.

"In terms of The Coliseum, back then, people thought it was a depressing place. It wasn't somewhere that you felt was exciting to play in, until that playoff game, where even the players were like, 'I've never heard this place like this.' It was intense.

"You could just tell, even during warm-ups. I remember how many times they were just glaring at each other (from across the ice). Guys like Webb and Eric Cairns, who was a big defenseman, were just glaring across the ice, letting guys know they were going to feel them tonight.

"I just remember, they (the Islanders) had a tough guy named Jim Cummins, who was another fourth-line type and didn't really play a lot. And I remember that Laviolette sent him out to take the opening face-off. Even the Leafs knew when they saw him why he was out there. He was not out there to score goals. It was just a tone setter from the very beginning because of how nasty Game 5 was. And so, already, there was just this feeling like your hair was standing up before the game even started.

"You could just tell this was going to be a brawl all-night long. And then, Webb's first shift, have you ever played pinball? I mean, he was just bouncing off walls and bouncing off people, just wrecking people. That's what he was.

"And remember, it was Gary Roberts who put the hit on Kenny Jonsson in Game 5 that gave him a concussion.

"So Webb put a hit on Gary Roberts and Roberts' skates went up in the air. That's how hard he hit him. He knocked him almost out of his skates and the place went nuts. And I remember the officials looked the other way, like there wasn't a penalty call, because it's almost as if the officials kind of knew to let them get their pound of flesh, because everybody saw what happened in Game 5.

"There was no replay back then. There was no way to check the video to see if something happened. That hit on Peca, it was behind the play. The official never saw it. So, because he didn't see it, there was no penalty and The League back then didn't do things where it would review and then assign supplemental discipline. They didn't do that. So he got away with a dirty hit and he was targeted, it was obvious.

"It was as if the officials were even kind of like, 'are you serious?' when Roberts got up after the hit and started yelling at them. They looked at him like, 'after what you did in Game 5, are you serious?' And once the Islanders took the lead, things got really nasty. It was as if the Leafs were trying to fight back a little bit.

"Webb went after Tucker a lot. He kept chasing him down because Webb and Peca were close. So there was a lot of that. Tucker wouldn't fight, he would just kind of duck out of hits, but he wouldn't fight. He just kept talking.

"Shayne Corson was one of the Leafs' tough guys and Corson also wasn't really interested in getting involved with anything, until, I guess, it just got so nasty that he had to. And Eric Cairns, who is about 6-6, 240 lbs., got a hold of him. And I mean, the beating he put on him, I've never seen anything like it.

"He just beat him right down to the ice. He had his gloves off, his jersey sleeves were up as if he had pushed his sleeves up before he started throwing. And he just absolutely mauled Corson all the way down. And as the crowd was cheering, Cairns skated to the tunnel, because he knew he was getting sent off. He had his fist in the air, like waving to the crowd and pumping and pointing his finger in the air and there was a loud ovation for that moment.

"At that point, you just knew there was going to be a Game 7."

While the final score of 5-3 doesn't really tell the tale of the game, it was actually 2-2 after the first period, as all the nastiness couldn't prevent these teams from putting pucks in the back of each other's nets. But once the second period came around, the scoring became one-sided (in the Isles' favor) and the game settled in; at least until six different players were assessed fighting majors near the end of the third period.

Corson, Cairns, Tucker, Bates, Cummins and Tie Domi all were assessed five-for-fighting in the waning minutes of the third period, to provide an added bit of zest to a game that had already been reminiscent of the "Bad Old Days," when brawls were a lot more commonplace.

But in the end all that mattered was that the Isles staved off elimination and had lived to fight again another day.

A PICTURE IS WORTH 1,000 WORDS

HAHN: "It's not a happy one. This was pretty serious, because it was the first day of Training Camp in 2001 and it happened to be 9/11. We were up in Lake Placid and I remember waiting for practice to begin. I was supposed to do a radio spot for a Long Island radio station and the guy called me and he goes, 'Hey, we're going to have to postpone it. There's some news, something happened in the city. I'll get back to you.' I said, 'okay.' And within five minutes there was now a buzz around the arena. We were up in Lake Placid in the rink where the U.S. won the gold medal in 1980. I mean, what a place to be and all of a sudden it was, 'Hey, we've got to get to a TV.'

"I stood in a room with pretty much the entire team, coaching staff, (Mike) Milbury and a bunch of writers and we watched The Towers fall on T.V. and there was silence in the room. There were a lot of Canadians, some Russians, some Swedes; it wasn't just a bunch of Americans. There was only, I think, two or three Americans on the team, but we all knew what that was about. And it's just, you know who you are. I'm a writer. You're the player. Like we know that and we didn't cross certain boundaries. We were never really buddies or friends. You're acquaintances. Over time you develop friendships -- later on. But when you're covering them, it's sort of like, 'I'm on this side, and you're on that side.'

"But that was the most unified (thing I've ever experienced). It was just a strange thing. We were all just people in a room watching something that changed the world and wondering what was going to happen next. It was a lot of fear. There were no cell phones where you could call home. There was a lot of fear. I mean, I couldn't call back to Long Island to check on anyone.

"We couldn't go home because we were informed that everything was closed. The bridges, the roads, everything, you couldn't go anywhere. So we were just stuck up there. It's not sports-related; obviously, it's not a moment on the ice. But for my career, it's a moment I'll never forget because of the way it happened and how it happened and the people I was with at the time. It's very much a moment and a day in my career that I'll never, ever forget."

12 SHANNON HOGAN (MSG NETWORK)
"JOHN TAVARES! AND THE 23-YEAR WAIT...IS...OVER!"
(@BARCLAYS CENTER)
APRIL 24, 2016
NYI 2, FLA 1 (2OT)

BACKGROUND

When it comes to sports broadcasts, fans can immediately name their favorite play-by-play announcers and color commentators. But there is usually a third party involved who perhaps isn't quite as well known, but certainly just as important -- the studio host!

The studio host has been around for decades but has only recently begun to gain more mainstream fandom. And in hockey the studio host is of utmost importance as they are the ones who give the viewers -- fans -- all the juicy information they need before the puck is ever dropped on the ice.

Plus, we currently live in an era where there are some really good hosts in hockey studios across the NHL. And one of the best happens to ply her craft for MSG Networks on their Islanders broadcasts. Of course, I'm talking about Shannon Hogan.

Hogan came to MSG in 2014 and almost overnight became a fan-favorite for her knowledge of the game and her ability to get the best information out of her guests. Whether that meant chatting with the team's beat writers, or some of her MSG colleagues, Hogan always got the fans ready for what awaited in that night's game. And she also happens to do the intermission reports, which, if you've ever had the opportunity to watch live from the arena, are truly a sight to behold as fans swarm to the guarded ropes in support of Hogan.

But how did this former-collegiate swimmer become such a hit in the NHL?

HOGAN: "I've always loved sports and it's been a big part of our family dynamic for as long as I can remember. My mom was a die-hard Ohio State fan. She went to Ohio State, so we grew up watching a whole lot of Ohio State football. My dad went to Gonzaga, so we were cheering for Gonzaga basketball. But I didn't fall in love with hockey until we moved to Detroit.

"We moved to Detroit in 1999, right in the middle of my sophomore year of high school and from there I ended up graduating and I was obviously a Red Wings fan. It was in the thick of Red Wings' Mania with the way they were continuing to make the playoffs every year.

"It was just an electric atmosphere and I'd never experienced anything like it. So I kind of got the hockey bug. I graduated high school in Northville, Michigan in 2003 and I went on to University of Virginia.

"I was on the swim team there and we won the ACC my freshman year. Eventually, after a year in the program there, I realized I did not want to go to grad school. I knew what I wanted to do and I needed a journalism degree. So I went to the world's first journalism school, the University of Missouri, and it was the best thing I could have done.

"It was an amazing experience and it totally prepared me with The Missouri Method to be in the world of journalism and also to do both sports and news.

"My first job out of college in 2008 was actually at KION radio, which is in Salinas, California. But I lived in Monterey and I was hired as their weekend sports anchor and weekday news reporter. They were supposed to hire a sports director and they didn't. So, it was just me, at 22; which was really wild. But I felt like Missouri did the best they could to prepare me for those kinds of situations and while I was over there I got to cover great events: the 2010 Giants World Series; AT&T Pebble Beach Pro-Am and the U.S. Open when Graeme McDowell won. So it really gave me a taste of what big sports were.

"And after two-years there, I got an opportunity with Fox Sports Detroit. I will never forget calling my mother to let her know I had an interview because I didn't want her to be excited since it was in Detroit. The chances of getting an opportunity to cover a team and cover sports at that level in your 'hometown,' or where your family lives, is slim to none, especially in your 20's. I called her and I was like, 'mom, don't get excited, but I have an interview with Fox Sports Detroit.' She was like, 'no, no, I won't get excited.'

"Then she got off the phone and she just started screaming. Luckily I ended up getting the job. I covered the Tigers, Red Wings and Pistons for four-years, which was a wonderful experience because it really taught me what I needed to know to host a show. And that kind of led me to the opportunity with MSG.

"I remember my agent calling and saying, 'I don't know if you'd be interested in this job, but it's pretty unique because there's no studio, so you'll have to do a lot of work.' And I said, 'I really want to do the work. I want to be responsible for content. I want to write things. I don't want somebody just to feed me things.' He said, 'well, it's with the New York Islanders. How do you feel about New York?' I said, 'I love New York, let's get an interview.' So I interviewed with the MSG, ended up getting the job in 2014 and was a little nervous.

"I wasn't 100% sure if it was going to be a forever thing, but after nine-months, that first season of covering the team, I sold my house in Michigan and was a New Yorker I guess. So that's how I got to the Islanders and it's been a wild ride.

"This is my 10th year in the NHL, which just seems crazy and the team has been so good to me. MSG has been so amazing and I've worked with a lot of the same crew for a long-time. Our producer Jim Gallagher has been the only voice in my ear for six-years now. And Charlie Cucchiara who does our tape is kind of my 'Go To Guy.' We do a lot of work before every game, going through the highlights, going through the video, going through the interviews.

"And then Joel Mandelbaum came on after Dave Hagen retired. Sarah Servetnick has been doing our graphics for the last several years and I had the opportunity to work with Howie Rose for a couple of years before Brendan Burke got hired. And Butch Goring too. So it's kind of been a dream job."

MOST UNFORGETTABLE ISLANDERS GAME

By the time the 2015-16 season came around, the Islanders had officially moved into a new home, Barclays Center in Brooklyn, NY and they were still carrying around a playoff series winless drought of 22-years and counting after being eliminated by Washington in the first-round back in April.

But October brought a renewed sense of purpose to the team. And the team rode that to another 100-point campaign; its second straight. However, getting through the regular-season was just part one of what they hoped was a multi-part play. So, after qualifying for the post-season, the question once again became, would this finally be the year the Islanders broke their drought and advanced beyond the opening-round?

It wouldn't be easy, but if any team could do it, it was this iteration of the Long Island-turned-Brooklyn boys.

The Isles first-round opponent was the Florida Panthers, a good team for sure, but one that the Islanders were plenty capable of beating. In fact, right out of the gate, the Islanders won Game 1 down in Florida before settling for a split thanks to a Game 2 loss and headed back to Brooklyn for their first ever playoff game at Barclays Center.

A Game 3 overtime victory had the Isles and their fans flying high, but a Game 4 loss brought them back to Earth as the series shifted back to Florida. And it was in Florida that young Alan Quine proved his mettle by scoring the game-winning goal in double-overtime to set the stage for a return to Brooklyn and a possible first-round series victory; something the Isles hadn't experienced since 1993.

Could the Islanders finally get over the hump? And more importantly, could they do it at home and avoid the potential pitfall that a Game 7 in Florida would be?

HOGAN: "Normally I get to the rink around the same time and I go to the truck to go through things. So, I kind of felt like it was business as usual that day, even though there was a lot of stuff going on.

"And I do remember that my mom had picked out my outfit, which was kind of strange to think back on, but I remember her going through my closet and labeling the clothes I was gonna wear for each game with a tag. Game 1, Game 2, etc. so that I had the perfect balance of Islanders blue.

"(Getting ready for that game) there were butterflies in my stomach and I actually can remember getting ready for pre-game that night and people would walk by our set. People were coming over and saying, 'tonight's the night Shannon, tonight's the night.' People just wanted it to happen so badly. They were trying to will it into existence. And a big part of that speaks to the identity of this group as fans, which is, they believe in the team.

"They are superstitious. I'm superstitious. Some reporters, some hosts are not, but I am. And I feel like they (the fans) have that feeling too. They were doing what they needed to do for the pre-game."

As excited and nervous as the Islanders fans and broadcasters were, they did have home-ice advantage and a quick start could be just what the doctor prescribed for those stomach butterflies. Unfortunately, Florida struck first when Jonathan Huberdeau scored with just 1:02

remaining in the first period to give the Panthers a 1-0 lead; as well as to give the home fans an all to familiar queasy feeling in their stomachs.

Surely somebody would step up and restore order for the Islanders, right? Um, maybe not.

As the game progressed the Islanders showed no ability to solve Panthers netminder Roberto Luongo, who was turning aside every one of the shots the Isles sent his way. And believe me, there were a lot of them.

No matter what the Isles tried, Luongo was at his very best and they just could not sneak one by him. And just as it looked like a Game 7 was indeed in the offing, Islanders captain John Tavares stepped up, beating Luongo with just 54-seconds remaining in the third period.

So there they were, the Islanders seemingly brought back from the dead were now heading to overtime with a new lease on life. But the first overtime period bore no winner, so the game advanced to double-overtime. And at that point, two things were crystal clear: 1) if the Islanders lost the game, it was going to be very difficult to rebound for Game 7 and 2) should the Isles pull off the win in Game 6, Barclays Center was going to come unglued with emotions.

And the fans sure hoped it would be Option Two. The question was, who could potentially step up and be the hero the Islanders needed?

HOGAN: "I remember, one thing I always do, Glenn Petraitis, who works with me as our stage manager, we didn't ever like to go down ice-side during a game unless there was five-minutes to go and the Islanders were in the lead, because I felt like I could end up jinxing it.

"So, I went down around the three-minute mark and I just remember standing there and my feet being freezing. Rick DiPietro was basically shifting his weight from side-to-side behind me, like he was playing in the game. It was like he was the backup goalie. I was so nervous watching him.

"I remember watching John Tavares during a commercial break and I mean, he was an intense guy to begin with, but there was something in his eyes. He was not letting that series go back to Florida. So it didn't surprise me at all that he was going to put the team on his back if he had to. And that was what made him so effective.

"We were at the far end of the ice so we could see John Tavares go for the wraparound. And it was like everything moved in slow-mo. For as quick as hockey is, it was almost like it was slow-down mode. It was almost like I could drown out the sound; like it was one buzz and they scored.

"As a journalist, you're not supposed to celebrate. But we had just gotten so wrapped up in the series and so wrapped up with the fans and the emotion. I think I was four-feet off the ground and I was hugging the Islanders massage therapist. I looked over behind me and Rick DiPietro was jumping up and down, hugging a security guard. It was wild. It was the loudest, most sustained cheer I'd ever heard in any sporting event.

"It was just a feeling of relief. I still have Goosebumps thinking about it now. It makes me so happy being back in that moment. I will never forget that feeling. The feeling of them winning was, I think I was proud. It had nothing to do with me, but I was proud for the team. It was a sense of pride. It was a sense of relief.

"I feel like you could hear the emotion rise and then almost everybody breathe. Unfortunately the second-round didn't go as well as they wanted, but it didn't matter at that point. It was like they just needed to get over that hump. I think that was the overwhelming feeling, of pride and relief."

A PICTURE IS WORTH 1,000 WORDS

HOGAN: "Have you ever seen a drone shot? I would like the biggest drone shot I could have of every single Islanders fan I've had the opportunity to meet. And every player I've had the opportunity to interview. As well, I'd have every person I've had the opportunity to work with, because that's what it takes to make a broadcast.

"This is going to sound crazy, but I'd like to have both Barclays and The Coliseum in it, because I think that's all a part of the story. And no matter how you feel about the arena situation, it's part of the journey and it's part of the story. But I would like one of those aerial photos in which you could see everybody's face. And I'd like to be surrounded by the fans, the players -- past and present -- and the great crew who I have the opportunity to work with, because without them, the product on the air doesn't happen."

13 ALLAN KREDA (NY TIMES)
GAME 6: 2015 EASTERN CONFERENCE FIRST-ROUND
(@NASSAU COLISEUM)
APRIL 25, 2015
NYI 3, WSH 1

BACKGROUND

New York City, specifically the borough of Brooklyn, is known for its deep love of sports. If you think about it, you can probably name dozens upon dozens of professional athletes, broadcasters and journalists alike, who trace their roots back to Brooklyn.

Just off the top of my head you have names like: Joe Torre, Stan Fischler, Carmelo Anthony, Phil Rizzuto and Sandy Koufax; the list goes on and on. And don't forget about ace NY Times reporter, Allan Kreda.

While many fans know Allan Kreda as the man who has covered the NY Rangers and NY Islanders for over a decade, they don't usually know that he almost didn't become a sports writer.

In fact, when Kreda was a student at CUNY Brooklyn College he wasn't even a journalism major. But that soon changed thanks to a single news writing class taught by Professor Bruce Porter.

"Porter, who was the leader of the journalism program at that time, took a liking to me and my writing," said Kreda. "And he suggested that for the next semester I should get an internship to obtain some experience in the field."

So, at the urging of Professor Porter, Kreda applied for and was granted an internship with a well-known alumnus of Brooklyn College, "The Hockey Maven," Stan Fischler.

"That was in 1985," Kreda explains. "And it's still going strong today. After many forms of my writing and going from *The Associated Press* to *Bloomberg News* to *The New York Times* currently and a host of magazines and other outlets in between, I've essentially been around the Rangers and Islanders in one form or another for 30 years."

KREDA: "(My Islanders coverage) is kind of in two parts, starting with my very early hockey experience as an intern for the Fischler machine back in the mid-80s. My first games were there at The Coliseum, for the most part, as part of the *SportsChannel* crew, pregame, post-game and between periods.

"So my earliest hockey media work entails the Islanders post-Cup group. I got to see (Bobby) Nystrom, (Clark) Gillies, (Denis) Potvin, etc. on the ice in those years. So, it came full circle when I had the chance to then cover the Islanders for the *New York Times* starting in 2013, which was basically a few months after it was announced the Islanders would be leaving Long Island for Barclays Center in Brooklyn in 2015; so there were three-seasons of the long goodbye and all that went with that."

With his wealth of experience guiding him, Allan Kreda has been a key witness to many memorable Islanders moments. But one stands out above the rest.

MOST UNFORGETTABLE ISLANDERS GAME

By the time the 2014-15 playoffs were underway the Islanders had gone almost 22-years without winning a single playoff series; with their last victory being against the Penguins in 1993.

And for a franchise with as proud and winning a tradition as the Islanders, that was a tough pill to swallow. But what was even tougher to swallow was that this was going to be the last time the Islanders ever played a game inside Nassau Coliseum, for they were moving to Brooklyn's Barclays Center at the start of the 2015-16 season and they were expected to be there for at least the next several decades.

The Coliseum had been at the heart of a vast majority of the Islanders iconic moments, but its days were numbered and had been for three-years. So, after a season that saw the franchise honor its long-time home several times, could the team send off The Old Barn with one more memorable moment?

If they were, it would have to come against the Washington Capitals, who presented quite the challenge as the Isles first-round opponent. Unfortunately, by the middle of the series, it was clear the Islanders were outmatched, so their hopes of ending 22-years of frustration were nigh.

In fact, because the Islanders had lost Game 4 at The Coliseum and then proceeded to drop Game 5 in D.C., it was very possible that Game 6 (back in Nassau) would indeed be the final game ever played at The Old Barn. For even if the Isles managed to pull off the win, they would still have to return to D.C. for Game 7, which was a daunting task in its own right.

At that point, many fans were more concerned with sending the building off with one last hurrah; more so than trying to keep the hope alive that the team could make it to the second-round. And it wasn't just the fans who felt this way as numerous reporters shared the sentiment and shaped their stories accordingly. One such reporter was Allan Kreda, who had longstanding ties to The Coliseum and was keenly aware of what Game 6 could mean.

KREDA: "There are many memorable games (in the Islanders' history), but since The Coliseum was such an emotional part of the team, of the psyche of the fans and of the ethos of the franchise, I do have strong memories of what was then called 'The Final Game.' We didn't know it at the time, but Game 6 against Washington in the first-round of the playoffs in 2015, was, of course, after the last regular-season game. In the playoffs, you don't know when the last game is actually the last game and this particular afternoon was one where the Islanders had to win to keep the series going.

"They were up against Alex Ovechkin and the Capitals; not an easy opponent. They played them pretty close, tooth and nail, back-and-forth. The emotion in the building was as strong as it's ever been.

"Game 6 stays with me because it sort of had everything The Coliseum was about: the loud, insane fans; the screaming sounds in the building; it was shaking every time the Islanders touched the puck. When they scored their three-goals, the emotions were just running high. The fans desperately wanted it all to continue and then the long good-bye was finally at an end.

"You rarely see three-years of something like that. At the time, if they had lost that game, they would have been in Brooklyn next year; notwithstanding what's happened in the past couple of years of going back and forth and with Belmont coming soon. But at the time, the feeling was this was all coming to an end.

"It was sad. It was really sad, I think, because the fans who were for long had tailgated and driven to the games and just very much made it a Long Island destination. The team was really about the area. That was the end of it. Brooklyn is not Long Island. It's not Manhattan. It's its own situation. No one knew what it would be like suddenly with most fans taking trains to games and just changing the entire dynamic; the home game experience to Brooklyn.

"Basically, they may as well have been moving to Kansas at that point, because it was really far away from everything familiar with the franchise and what it had been for 43-years. So it was just sad. I think the buildup was really long. It was too long. And when it was finally at the end, the fans were more missing the building then sad for the season going away. And at that time, it seemed like Brooklyn was going to be their home for the next 25-years, at least and there would never be another game on Long Island.

"The Islanders had a good team that year. They were led by John Tavares. He got them to the playoffs. They hadn't won a series since 1993, which was hanging over their heads the whole way. They had come close in 2013 against Pittsburgh, but couldn't get past the Penguins in a very hard fought first-round, which really cemented The Coliseum as a destination for playoff games again. And then, you come to 2015, where they seemed to have the horses to upend the Caps, but just not quite enough.

"Jack Capuano coached them well. They had a lot of talent, but it just wasn't enough. It was more sadness for the end of the building and the end of an era and for so many fans, it was basically the end of it all.

"(Going into the game) everything was about the next game and focusing on the next 60-minutes. Plus, it was an afternoon game, Game 6. So, there was no morning skate. It was really just coming off Game 5, the Islanders knew they had to win or it was over. You sort of had the sense they weren't going to let it end with a loss, because everyone knew it could be the end of the building. So there seemed to be super effort to make sure that didn't happen.

"You could feel it throughout the lead up to the game. And the game, of course, itself was very, very close.

"I'm pretty sure that Capuano started (Casey) Cizikas, (Matt) Martin and (Cal) Clutterbuck. They sort of did that every game. That would always get the crowd going, because there would always be some sort of hit off the face-off; some physicality to begin the pace of the game. With the Caps and the way they played, they were at each other from the moment the puck dropped; there was no shortage of physical skirmishes, battles.

"So, I'm sure there was something right off the face-off and the roar really never stopped. A relentless 60-minutes was what the Islanders were going to give that afternoon. There was no question that was coming. So, when they did score, when John Tavares scored early in the game that really got everything off on the right foot for the team. They played their usual steady defense, their playoff-style kept the lead.

"Then the Caps actually tied it with five-seconds left in the first period. So, that slightly took the air out of everybody going into the break.

"You couldn't expect to shut out the Caps. They were not going to go quietly, obviously. So, them scoring was not a surprise. It was just; the tension got ratcheted up a little more because, surely, if they went ahead, that wouldn't be good. That wouldn't be helping the cause. The Islanders knew they had to play it close. And what was interesting about that game was that Colin McDonald, who was a fan favorite three-years earlier when they played the Penguins, he was back. He actually played in this game and he helped set the tone to a large degree.

"And then you had a second period that went back-and-forth, but no goals were scored. So obviously, going into the third period, the feeling was, the next goal wins. It was already overtime at that point. Obviously you weren't going to see a 6-1 game at that juncture. So the tension was thick and it was just a matter of what play was going to break the ice. And it happened at 10:33 when Kulemin got the goal. It was actually assisted by (Nick) Leddy and Tavares.

"It was a workmanlike goal. For Kulemin, it was a big moment. He hadn't scored a lot of goals in his career. So that was a major moment for him. It was just a workmanlike, Islander-type goal that was born out of the style that Capuano professed them to play.

"I remember clearly that they were not going to let the lead go away. They were going to kill themselves on the ice to make sure it didn't stop. Anything goes (at that point). Blocking shots, taking the body, within reason, no penalties. But they were not going to let the lead go at that point. 2-1 with nine-minutes left. They were making sure they got the 'W.'

"Then, when Cal Clutterbuck got the puck in his own end and fired it down for the empty-net, that was a moment of pure excitement and thrill, because the game was over; basically. Everyone could go home happy, at least for that afternoon. No matter what, the Islanders had to win that proverbial final game. It was absolute tension and angst up until the 19:07 mark when Clutterbuck, the prototypical Islander, got the goal and cemented the win, 3-1 to send it back to Washington for Game 7 two-days later.

"The feeling I had was that they won this game and whatever happens in Game 7, they've gone out with the exact right effort. So, no matter what would happen, if this was the end of the series, they had ended The Coliseum with a win.

"And post-game, I do remember Capuano saying that the fans had been like a sixth man to the team and that they practically willed them to victories in big games; especially playoff games. So, he was pointed in thanking the fans for what they brought energy-wise and how they lifted the club before the game and during warm-ups. It was an all-day thing. The roar never stopped."

A PICTURE IS WORTH 1,000 WORDS

KREDA: "It would probably be John Tavares celebrating his double-overtime winning goal against Florida in 2016, which was the Islanders' first year in Brooklyn, which is when the Islanders finally won a series for the first time since 1993. The wait was exceptionally long. They came close in '13, but in '16, they surmounted the challenge, finally; some histrionics along the way. But I think, with John Tavares, with all he had given to the franchise since he was the first overall pick in 2009, and he finally won a series seven years later, it was a long road.

"He went through a lot to get there. He deserved that moment for himself and for the franchise. The image of him scoring, which was right below the press view at Barclays Center, it was pure exultation, a pure thrill of the moment. It was double-overtime in Game 6, which meant they didn't have to go back and play a Game 7 in Florida. So if there is a moment of my career and there are many good ones, that would be the pinnacle one."

14 STEVE MEARS (WBBR/WMJC)
AL ARBOUR 1,500 (@NASSAU COLISEUM)
NOVEMBER 3, 2007
NYI 3, PIT 2

BACKGROUND

Ever since the Islanders joined the NHL, they have been blessed with a terrific lineage of stellar broadcasters.

From Jim Gordon to Spencer Ross to Steve Albert and Al Albert, to John Sterling, Jiggs McDonald, Barry Landers, Howie Rose, Chris King and Brendan Burke, the Islanders have had no shortage of television and radio broadcasters who have been at the top of their profession. There's even a few Hall of Famers in there.

And one name who belongs on that list is current Penguins broadcaster and one-time Isles radio man, Steve Mears.

Mears had the unfortunate task of calling Islanders games at a time when the franchise was going through a transitional period; so, many fans don't like to look back on those years with any sort of fondness.

But from 2006-2009, Mears brought a level of excellence to the Islanders radio booth that helped catapult his career to new heights. And his contributions to Isles broadcasts won't be forgotten anytime soon by the fans who stuck with the team during the hard times.

Even now, with Mears back home in Pittsburgh calling games for his hometown Penguins, he still gets a well deserved cheer from the Islanders fans who he comes across when the Pens and Isles faceoff.

But how did this lad from Pittsburgh end up in New York, living out Frank Sinatra's "if you can make it here, you can make it anywhere"?

MEARS: "I grew up in Pittsburgh as a lifelong Penguins fan. And at the time, when I was growing up, at that very impressionable age of 10 or 11, the Penguins had the best player in Mario Lemieux. They had a team that won back-to-back Stanley Cups and they had the best announcer in Mike Lange, a Hall of Famer.

"I just simply wanted to be like him. I thought it was the greatest job in the world. He got in for free. He got paid to be there. He got to talk about the games and bring the games to life; to a live audience. And that was the appeal for me.

"From that age on, it was all about taking the necessary steps to try to do this for real, to do it for a living. I was able to go to a good broadcasting college -- Bowling Green -- and work in Minor League Hockey.

"I was in the Central Hockey League, which was a Double-A league that no longer exists. But it was a very good league. It was in Louisiana. I went from college; I graduated, packed up my car and moved down to Louisiana after I got the job. And it was the best four years I could ever ask for.

"It was like getting my Master's (degree) in hockey and sports, because you learned every aspect of what it means to be in the sports business. Broadcasting was actually a very small part of that job. So I had the chance to learn about the business side. I did sales. I did media relations, community relations and team relations.

"Then, when 7 o'clock rolled around, there was a little bit of time to prepare and I called the game. It really helped sharpen all of my skills; everything that I needed to become a good broadcaster and just a sports businessperson. At that point, I was then lucky enough to get my big break, which was getting a job doing radio for the New York Islanders. And that was a perfect first NHL job.

"Even though I was really young -- 26 during the 2006-07 season -- it was a perfect place to start out in The League, because the team was young and just living on Long Island, it was wonderful. And I was with the Islanders from 2006-07 to 2008-09."

MOST UNFORGETTABLE ISLANDERS GAME

For as many beloved figures as there are throughout the history of the New York Islanders, one stands out from the rest. And that is legendary coach Al Arbour.

Arbour was the third-ever coach in Isles history, taking over at the start of their second season (1973-74) and remaining behind the bench until the conclusion of the 1985-86 campaign. And then, he even turned in a second tour of duty with the team from midway through the 1988-89 season until he hung 'em up for good after the 1993-94 campaign.

During his two tours as Islanders Head Coach, Arbour racked up 1,499 games coached, 739 wins and four Stanley Cup championships. A full career indeed and one that landed him in the Hall of Fame.

But even with all of his accomplishments there was something missing. And it wasn't even Arbour himself who thought there was something missing, rather, it was Isles Head Coach Ted Nolan, who stood behind the Isles bench from 2006-2008.

During Nolan's brief tenure with the team he would frequently walk through the hallways inside Nassau Coliseum and see that there was a plaque on one of the walls that commemorated Arbour's career with the team by highlighting his total of 1,499 games coached. And during the summer of 2007, Nolan was struck by an inspiration, one that would lead to a third -- yet brief -- tour of duty for Arbour with the Islanders.

MEARS: "Ted Nolan, it was really his idea. He saw the plaque on the wall in the hallway at Nassau Coliseum and saw it said 1,499. He wanted that round number of 1,500. So he said to Garth Snow, 'why not bring Al back?'"

With that idea, Nolan then reached out to Arbour and "Radar" was on board. Now the question was when to do it? Eventually, it was decided that November 3, 2007, against the Penguins at Nassau Coliseum would be the site of Arbour's return. So, Al signed a one-day contract with the team to return to the bench one final time -- at the age of 75 -- as the franchise prepared to honor it's greatest coach.

Could the modern day Isles make it a victorious return?

MEARS: "It was just such a magical night, just to be around Al and I got a chance to do a sit down interview with him to hear his stories about the dynasty-era and the way the players embraced him. And he embraced the role (too).

"It wasn't like it was just some kind of photo op and it was all fluff. He really wanted to win and he wanted to help the team in any way he could. It was like we all stepped into a time machine. He went right back to his position on the bench at Nassau Coliseum, circa 1982. And it was just so magical the entire night, the way Ted Nolan worked with Al and the way they communicated with each other.

"(I sat down with Al) before the game and it was in The Coliseum, at one of the lounges, I think or the suite level. One of the things I remember is, I asked Al what was the most memorable exchange he ever had with an official and he told me the story. I don't remember the specifics of the story now, but I remember laughing hysterically at his answer because you can imagine the exchanges he had. He had so many good stories and you could just sit there for hours (with him).

"I'm a hockey nerd. I love talking with the greats of the game, talking about the sport and then some of the strategy and the history of the game. So, to be around Al and just to have, whatever it was, maybe 10 minutes, of a sit down conversation for Islanders TV, that was really, really cool. I remember sitting there thinking and looking at him, he was wearing those glasses and I was just thinking, 'this is the coolest thing in the world. I'm sitting here and across from me is one of the greatest coaches of all-time.'

"On radio that night, my partner Chris King and I would give some anecdotes, but it was just a hockey game on radio. On TV it would have been different. And Chris, he's basically been there since Day One in 1972. So, to have his historical perspective, where I didn't have as much to offer simply because I wasn't alive, as a kind of a historical guide along the way. I know he brought so much to that broadcast that night.

"And then the way the game unfolded in dramatic fashion "

The Isles fell behind 2-0 early on goals from Ryan Malone (first period) and Tyler Kennedy (second period), so things didn't look good. And to compound the issue, Isles netminder Rick DiPietro was forced from the game midway through the second period after getting cut by Sidney Crosby's stick. The Isles then sent Wade Dubielewicz into the net and he finished out the game.

Shortly before Dubielewicz came in, Trent Hunter had sliced the Isles deficit in half, but the team still headed into the third period down by a goal and time was running out to make Arbour's return a winning one.

And then came the Miroslav Satan show. With 5:30 gone by in the third, Satan scored an emphatic goal to tie the game and bring the crowd to its feet. His goal even got a double-arm raise from Arbour himself on the bench. But a tie game is not a win; so another goal was still needed. And once again Satan came through, netting the eventual winner with just 2:41 left on the clock.

MEARS: "Miro Satan scored late in the game, the Islanders won it and the place went crazy. That roar from the crowd, it was just a wonderful night all around and a celebration of one of the greatest coaches in NHL history and one of the great figures in Islanders history.

"We all knew, no matter how the game unfolded, it was going to be a truly special night to have him standing there on the bench. And then, to have it be a dramatic win on top of all that, it just all culminated into one of the most memorable nights of my career.

"Al is a winner, one of the great winners in hockey history. I think the way the players responded and whatever strategy, or any type of hands on coaching, Al had to offer that night; it really wasn't the main storyline. It was more about a celebration of his great career and the fact that everyone was so receptive to his presence, that milestone and ultimately getting the win for him.

"I think, at the end, when the clock ticked down, my call was something along the lines of, 'Al Arbour has his 740th victory as a head coach with the New York Islanders.' To say those words really meant a lot, because it's an amazing win total. And to know that it was 1,500 games, that was awesome.

"And then, I remember them raising the banner, the Al Arbour 1,500 banner. It was hovering above the ice and the Islanders players, Ted Nolan and Al all got around and posed for a picture with the banner."

That banner still hangs proudly to this day as a constant reminder of the Isles and Arbour's greatness.

A PICTURE IS WORTH 1,000 WORDS

MEARS: "It would probably be the fact that I called my first NHL game with the Islanders and it was in October 2006, in Arizona. I was thinking, being in that broadcast booth, that this was a lifelong dream, just to be in that broadcast booth looking out at an NHL arena.

"So I was in an NHL broadcast booth and I was getting ready to do my first game and Wayne Gretzky was on the bench as the coach of the Coyotes. I think that one image of looking out at the ice and feeling like, 'I made it as an NHL broadcast.' I was really young and still had a lot to learn, probably didn't realize how much I still had to learn at the time, but I had a lot to learn.

"But just to look out at that ice and to see an NHL arena from that perspective and to know this was a lifelong dream that I had fulfilled was really, really cool. And I was fortunate because Jiggs McDonald was on the other side doing TV.

"He was filling in for Howe Rose, who was doing the Mets at the time as they were in the playoffs. So Jiggs McDonald was doing the television and another image that will always stay with me is of driving with Jiggs on the bus to go to the game. I was there with this Hall of Fame announcer, who I always looked up to, with a great voice and one of the best to ever do it.

"To have Jiggs there with me to kind of show me the ropes and give me a little bit of advice (it meant a lot). I remember he said, 'always remember, it takes two teams to play this game.' So, I still remember to this day, that advice from Jiggs. He's always been someone who's really special to me."

15 BARRY MEISEL (NY DAILY NEWS)
THIS GAME WILL LAST FOREVER! THE EASTER EPIC
(@CAPITAL CENTER)
APRIL 18, 1987
NYI 3, WSH 2 (4OT)

BACKGROUND

Growing up you are always advised to chase your dreams. And that your dreams should always be realistic. But there are many, who for one reason or another, don't get to see their dreams to the finish line.

However, when you get to achieve your dream, it can be rather special. And that's exactly what New York City native, Barry Meisel managed to do.

Meisel grew up in an era when the media was probably more prominent than it had ever been and it inspired him to one day join the ranks of the reporters he admired growing up. But rather than become a news reporter, Meisel wanted to become a sports reporter, something that merged two interests of his; writing and sports.

For Meisel, this was a dream he would need to chase without any help from built-in connections. And that's what made it all the sweeter when he clawed his way to the top of the market.

MEISEL: "I was a high school student and I grew up during the Watergate era. I was fascinated by the Watergate hearings and the work of (Bob) Woodward and (Carl) Bernstein from *The Washington Post*. It made me want to be a writer, to be a reporter and I also loved sports. So, I figured in high school, what better way to put my two loves together of sports and writing. That's what got me started.

"I always believed and my professors and my teachers told me, 'take journalism courses and write.' I took internships. I wrote a lot of papers. I decided I wanted to be a sports writer.

"I grew up in New York City. Being a New Yorker, I wanted to work for one of the big papers in New York and my goal was, not unlike a player, to work my way up the system. Hockey was my first love. I went to school in upstate New York at Binghamton State and got a job for the local paper covering a Minor League Hockey team, the Broome Dusters.

"I worked my way up and applied for any open job. I took a step from Binghamton's *Sun Bulletin* to Morristown New Jersey's *Daily Record,* where I covered the Devils and Rangers. And then I was hired by the *New York Daily News* in October of 1985 to cover the Islanders.

"I actually covered the Islanders in Morristown at *The Record* in '84-'85; I was covering all of the local hockey teams. But I became the number one beat guy for the *New York Daily News* in the 1985-86 season and did hockey for five-seasons at the *Daily News*."

MOST UNFORGETTABLE ISLANDERS GAME

When it comes to the list of the longest games in NHL history, you would be remiss if you did not mention the fabled "Easter Epic," which started on Saturday night April 18, 1987 and ended on Sunday morning April 19, which just so happened to be Easter Sunday.

MEISEL: "I was one of the writers who covered that game and I was the writer who called it the 'Easter Epic' that next morning, because the game started on Saturday night and it went so long that it went into Sunday morning, which was Easter Sunday."

This incredible game between the Islanders and the Capitals was so legendary that it led a coach from another team to boldly declare that he didn't need to know who won, because his team would now have the advantage in the next round of the playoffs. And by the way, that coach was Mike Keenan.

MEISEL: "One thing I remember is that Mike Keenan, who was the coach of the Philadelphia Flyers at the time, they had won their series and would play the winner of the Islanders-Capitals. And I remember talking to Keenan during one of the intermissions. He left after the first or second overtime, because he said, 'I don't need to know who wins this series. Now I've got a big advantage. I'm playing a team who no matter what is going to be exhausted."

It was a rather boastful declaration by Keenan and maybe a tad out of character. Or, then again, seeing as how Keenan had a reputation for chaos and being iron-willed, maybe it suited him just perfectly. But I digress. Let's get back to the game.

MEISEL: "The Capitals and Islanders had just started having a playoff history. The Islanders were coming off of the four-Cups and their 'Drive for Five.' They were no longer Stanley Cup champions and they had lost to the Capitals the year prior. And 1987 was the third-straight year the Islanders were playing the Capitals.

"They went down three-games-to-one and then won Games 5 and 6. So, coming back from a 3-1 deficit and going into Game 7, everyone knew Game 7 was going to be a fantastic game. As I recall, the Islanders played without a couple of key players. I'm pretty sure (Mike) Bossy was hurt and didn't play. And I also think Denis Potvin didn't play. The Islanders were pretty banged up for that Game 7. So it was a remarkable game even before it went to overtime.

"I (don't exactly remember) what I wrote about (before the game). But, knowing myself and knowing the importance of the game, I'm pretty confident I wrote about the fact that the Islanders were going to be without Bossy and Potvin and without a couple of key players it was going to be pretty remarkable if they could finish off this comeback from three-games-to-one given that Game 7 was in Washington. Of course, I'm sure I also referenced the other series they played the years before.

"It was just a great game. Game 7 is (usually) like that. Teams don't want to take a lot of chances. As I recall, it was a close game that went back and forth. I believe the Islanders were trailing by a goal and (Bryan) Trottier tied it. I remember there was a lot of tension in the building and a lot of tension on the ice because of the stakes and the fact that it was a close game. Both goaltenders were fantastic. Bob Mason (Capitals) and Kelly Hrudey for the Islanders were great. And it ended up being that Hrudey made history. He stopped 73 of 75 shots.

"It was one of the most fun nights of my life as a reporter. It was a Saturday night into Sunday and the *New York Daily News* was one of the biggest papers in the country at the time. Our deadlines were early, so I was on the phone with my editor at the desk in New York for two-hours straight, because with the deadline being so tight and the game was so important and being in overtime, I didn't have time to constantly update my story on the computer. We were literally updating it sentence-by-sentence as the game went on.

"I remember that I constantly asked my editor how many papers were going to have the updated story, because 11 o'clock became 12 o'clock and then became 1 o'clock (before the game ended). The game ended at 1:58 in the morning and the way it worked was the newspaper, the printing press was running all-night.

"So what they were going to do was stop the press and redo the game story when the game was over. So all-night, I was giddy saying, 'how many people are gonna read the story in the morning?' We did get it. I can't tell you how many (papers actually had a game story), it was a very small percentage, but my story did get into the paper the next morning.

"The most important thing from that game was the fact that by the third and fourth overtimes, remember it was April, the building was hot and the players were so tired that shifts became, go up the ice one time, go down the ice one time and get off the ice. It became literally a game of attrition.

"On the final play, Gord Dineen and Ken Leiter, were the two defensive defensemen who were on when the puck was shot in. The shot was blocked and came out to Pat LaFontaine, who was the Islanders best player and was pretty far away (from the net). But he took a shot that fooled Bob Mason; I'm not sure if Mason saw it and just beat him for the winning goal.

"It was kind of a broken play. There were so many broken plays, because, at that point, guys would just throw in the puck to the net and would hope something would happen. I think Mason was screened on the play.

"And after the game, I knew I had to do two things for the paper that night, even though very few people were going to read it. I had to put it in perspective. I had to quickly get on the phone and just dictate a couple of sentences to my editor to get the story in the paper that night. And so I did. I think at the time it was the fifth-longest game in NHL history. I described the goal. I talked about the phenomenal importance of winning a Game 7 on the road. And I quickly talked about the fact that the next round was starting less than two days later.

"I mean, there was a day off between games, but the Islanders, because the game went to 2 o'clock in the morning, they were losing half of one of their days off. Then, the important thing for me to do was to get down to the locker room. Knowing this was such a historic game. Knowing I'd have to write another story the next day for the entire press run and kind of recap the whole night and put it into perspective.

"That was one of my most fun post-game interview locker rooms because there were so many thousands of questions I had. I was asking guys how many sticks they used? How many jerseys? How much weight did they lose? I was asking questions that you wouldn't ask in a normal game. It was just such an unusual game."

A PICTURE IS WORTH 1,000 WORDS

MEISEL: "It would have to be a picture of the Islanders veterans, knowing that they were not going to win The Cup again. I covered the team after their fantastic dynasty run of four-straight Cups, their unsuccessful 'Drive for Five' and 19-straight series victories. I think they would never admit it at the time, but Billy Smith, (Mike) Bossy, (Bryan) Trottier, (Denis) Potvin, (Bob) Nystrom and (Clark) Gillies, deep down in their hearts, they knew their run was over.

"The Oilers had replaced them as the NHL's best team. The Oilers were starting their own dynasty. Looking back at it, I covered a group of proud champions after their time was done. They were still an incredible team. They were still making the playoffs. But I think they knew deep down in their heart of hearts they weren't going to win another Stanley Cup."

16 BOBBY NYSTROM (NY ISLANDERS)
GAME 2 OF THE 1980 SEMI-FINALS (@BUFFALO MEMORIAL
AUDITORIUM)
MAY 1, 1980
NYI 2, BUF 1 (2OT)

BACKGROUND

From 1975-1984, the New York Islanders were one of, if not, the best teams in the entire NHL. They won four-straight Cups from 1980-83. And they did it by epitomizing what it means to be a team.

Sure, they had Hall of Fame talent. Mike Bossy and Denis Potvin were two of the best to ever play their respective positions. And, of course, they had Al "Radar" Arbour behind the bench and Bill "Bow-Tie Bill" Torrey running things behind the scenes.

But they also had a gritty element that other teams just couldn't match. And one of their grittiest players was a Stockholm, Sweden native by the name of Bobby Nystrom.

The 6-1 right-winger had as much heart as anybody in the NHL and it was his physical brand of hockey that gave the Islanders an added dimension that so few other teams possessed. And he was rewarded for his will power with two iconic moments during a career that spanned from 1972 (he was part of the Isles inaugural season) to 1986.

The first moment was his double-overtime game-winning goal against Buffalo in Game 2 of the 1980 Semi-Finals. As for the other? Well, he scored the Stanley Cup-winning overtime goal in Game 6 of the

1980 Cup Final against Philadelphia; giving the Islanders their FIRST Stanley Cup championship.

Nystrom is a man of few words, preferring to let his actions speak for him. So, if any of you were wondering how he ended up as a New York Islander, here's the (short) story.

NYSTROM: "I just played hockey because I really, really enjoyed it. I was scouted by a gentleman who lived in the neighboring town and he recommended this junior team, the Calgary Centennials take a look at me.

"I was told a 1,000 times when I was playing with Calgary that I would never make it. My coach said, 'you might be a good Minor Leaguer if you fight more.' So, I was pretty surprised when I was the first guy drafted off our team.

"He (my coach) was a real tough customer and I'm not sure whether he was using reverse psychology or not. But, I was certainly pissed off at him; let's put it that way. His name was Scotty Munro. However, he was the first person who called and congratulated me (when I was drafted). I think it was really more to motivate me than anything else."

Well, I guess the motivation worked, because Nystrom's name is synonymous with the Islanders success. And truthfully, I can think of worse ways for someone to be remembered.

MOST UNFORGETTABLE ISLANDERS GAME

The 1979-80 season was a coming of age for the Islanders. Yes, the team had already risen to the top of The League in the handful of years prior, but this was different. The Isles needed to get over the hump and go from being a great team to being champions.

And they had just the group of players to do so. It was just a matter of whether or not they could apply the lessons they'd learned from their previous playoff failures.

NYSTROM: "We had such a major disappointment the year before, in that we won the President's Cup. We led The League (in points) and then we got into the playoffs and we were beaten by the Rangers.

"So, that was really, really disheartening for us. There's no question about it. But, we were having a pretty good year (in 1980), not as good as in '79, but in '80 we had a pretty solid record. Once we got in the playoffs, we just had a little bit more confidence. We were just a little bit more sure of ourselves than we were the prior year.

"The interesting thing was, we had to go through a couple rounds before we got to that point. The fact was we started off against L.A. and we got a couple big goals and ended up winning the series. It was a little touch-and-go there for a bit, but we ended up winning.

"(In my opinion) the most important series was the Boston series that followed. Clark Gillies and I were watching the sportscasters and they said the Bruins were going to just run us right out of the building. And we kind of made a pact, Clark and I that we weren't going to back off. Those first couple of games, it got pretty rough.

"We had a big brawl in one game. And we ended up winning the series because we stood up to the Bruins. And that gave us a lot of confidence, because we could play any style. Clark fought Terry O'Reilly, I don't know how many times. I fought John Wensick. Garry Howatt fought Wayne Cashman. We really came together in that series. I thought that was really an important thing.

"(Then) the series against Buffalo was, I'm not gonna say it was easy. I mean, no game in the playoffs is easy. But, the thing was, that coming out of the Boston series, we thought we might be able to intimidate them. We wanted to try to hold them down and maybe try to intimidate them a little bit. That series was a little bit different. We were pretty confident that we could beat them."

The Isles certainly held the Sabres down in Game 1, as they raced out to a quick lead in the series, courtesy of a 4-1 win at the Buffalo Memorial Auditorium. And that win gave the Islanders some welcome momentum as they looked to capture Game 2 in Buffalo and hopefully head home up 2-0 in the series.

But before they could snag that coveted 2-0 lead, they had to fight tooth and nail against the pesky Sabres, who wanted no part of another loss.

The teams played a fairly ordinary first period, but when the second period began, things got chippy. Nine different penalties were called during the period and were assessed to eight different players. But, luckily for the Islanders, the only thing that really mattered was goals. And deadline acquisition, Butch Goring saw to it that the Isles got what they needed as his tally at 15:02 of the second period gave the Isles a hard-fought 1-0 lead.

Then it was onto the third period, with the Isles hoping to close the game out in short order. Unfortunately, Buffalo's new "big line" of Gilbert Perreault, Rick Martin and Andre Savard conspired against the Isles to tie the game at the 11:47 mark of the third period. Savard, who was one of the replacements for René Robert on what had been known as

"The French Connection Line," netted the goal and ended up forcing the game into overtime.

NYSTROM: "We all felt really confident for overtime for some reason. I'm not sure why. Every time we would go into the end of third period we had the intermission (prior to overtime), someone would always yell out, 'Hey, who's going to be the hero?' And everyone in the room would say, 'I am, I am, I'm going to score the goal. I want to score the goal.'

"Al Arbour had taught us, don't be afraid to lose. But, be afraid to sit on your heels and be conscious or thinking that you're going to lose or make a mistake. What you'd rather do is be on your toes and attack and attack and attack and think that you're going to be the guy who's the hero at the end of the game. So he kind of drilled that into us. So, we were pretty confident."

But a single overtime wasn't enough, so the game headed to double-overtime.

NYSTROM: "Anytime you go through a whole overtime period, that in itself is pretty amazing, because normally, one team or the other scores fairly quickly.

"But that was a pretty tight game that we are playing and the fact was that (the way the winning-goal was scored) it was kind of a strange play really, because the shot came from the point. It kind of came around the net. I mean, it wasn't even on the net, but it bounced in such a way that it came right out to me. I was just standing right in front of the goaltender, trying to screen him, it came right out to me and I was able to just put it by him."

At the 1:20 mark of the second overtime, Nystrom delivered a well-deserved victory to his Islanders brothers and put the team up 2-0 in the series as it headed home for Game 3.

A PICTURE IS WORTH 1,000 WORDS

NYSTROM: "It would be of John Tonelli coming over with his stick and his glove and everything is flying off as he's coming to congratulate me on scoring the goal (1980 Stanley Cup-winning goal). And then I was absolutely mobbed by the rest of the players. I mean, I actually have that photo and it's absolutely a classic."

17 HOWIE ROSE (FOX SPORTS NET NEW YORK)
"BATES AGAINST JOSEPH...BATES IN ON GOAL...HE SHOOTS...HE
SCORES!"
(@NASSAU COLISEUM)
APRIL 24, 2002
NYI 4, TOR 3

BACKGROUND

Howie Rose was born in Brooklyn, NY, and from an early age, he knew he wanted to be a sports broadcaster.

"I'd probably known from a very early age that I wanted to get into broadcasting on some level," said Rose. "It always appealed to me. But in terms of hockey, the Rangers and broadcasting hockey for the Rangers, that was all because of Marv Albert. I fell in love with the Rangers and with the concept of broadcasting hockey all at the same time through Marv. It was 1966, when I was 12-years-old. The 1966-67 season was the first time the Rangers were in the playoffs after about a five-year absence."

"They didn't really generate a whole lot of attention in the newspapers back then," continued Rose. "But, around mid-November of that 1966-67 season, they started to play really well and they were generating more headlines and getting more attention. Then, one night, I happened to be stumbling around the radio dial and I came across WHN, 1050 AM New York, and Marv was doing a Rangers game. I stayed with it and was absolutely blown away. I was just completely enthralled by the excitement of it; by Marv, his pace, inflection, and obvious love for the Rangers. I was sucked in from that very moment."

So, at the tender age of 12, Howie Rose already knew what he wanted to do with his life; quite the amazing feat considering most take years to figure out their future endeavors.

Following the 1966-67 season, in late August of 1967, Rose came up with the idea to create the Marv Albert Fan Club. And when he mentioned it to his friends they quickly came on board. And that's really where the story of Howie Rose begins to gain traction.

"I said, 'Well, I guess we should get Marv's permission somehow,'" Rose recalled. "I looked up the phone number for WHN and called. The switchboard operator answered the phone and in my rather high-pitched adolescent voice, I said, 'is there some way I could possibly speak to Marv Albert? Please.' And the next thing I know, bang, he's on the line and I was nervous as all hell."

"I asked him if we could have his permission to start a fan club," said Rose. "He was so gracious and so generous with his time and his resources. He told us that if we ever wanted to come up and see WHN we could and if there's anything we needed to help make the fan club of success, he'd do it."

Whether it was sending photos to the new fan club or providing tickets to Rangers, Mets, or Yankees games, Marv Albert stuck to his promise. And a few years later, he would prove to be instrumental in starting Howie Rose's career. As Rose matured, Albert would listen to and critique his tapes. And as Rose tells it, Albert wouldn't just say, "This is good." Rather, he'd give constructive criticism of Rose's work. And that benefitted Howie greatly.

But the student-teacher relationship didn't stop there. In 1975 Rose formally began his career by working for Sports Phone. And two years later, he landed his first radio job with WHN, which had -- in Rose's words -- "been sort of Marv Albert's alma mater." Eventually, Rose began to build a name for himself. And when Marv's schedule began to cause him to miss some games, he would recommend Rose as his fill-in.

According to Rose: "because I had no track record, no resume of doing major league level play-by-play, it took a while for people at The Garden to kind of take a leap of faith on me. But Marv finally convinced them to do that."

Then, on January 24, 1985, Rose finally got to the chance to call his first Rangers game, a contest that they won 3-1 against the Detroit Red Wings. Ever since that night, Rose has been a fixture in broadcast booths across the New York sports scene.

And along the way he became friends with many media members, which is very important, because after leaving the Rangers after roughly a decade, it was his connections that helped Rose to land his gig with the Islanders.

ROSE: "Well, I had gotten wind of the fact through some channels within the business that, it looked like Jiggs (McDonald) wasn't going to be back. And so when I found out that he wasn't going to come back, I said to my agent right away, 'get on this.' You have to remember, at the time, even though I was doing the Rangers, I wasn't doing every game. I was probably doing three-quarters of them.

"It was a combination of wanting to get my own full-time play-by-play gig and getting a shot at doing television, which I'd done on a very limited basis up to then. Combine that with the fact the Islanders were so close to where I lived, on Long Island, that it just made all the sense in the world and we went after it."

And so, Rose's career on Long Island began during the 1995-96 season and carried him through the 2015-16 campaign.

MOST UNFORGETTABLE ISLANDERS GAME

In sports, play-by-play announcers can spend years, if not entire careers, searching, hoping for that one magical call that will last a lifetime. Some get it and others don't. But Howie Rose is special in that he's made a career out of uttering magical, timeless calls. And it just so happens that one of his biggest was during his time with the Islanders, when they played host to the Toronto Maple Leafs for Game 4 of their Eastern Conference Quarter-Finals series in 2002.

ROSE: "The 2001-02 season was my favorite of the 21-years I was with the Islanders because they broke through after having been out of the playoffs for seven-years in a row. It was the first-year they made the playoffs since I had become their television announcer.

"That series was just a battle, a blood war between the Islanders and Maple Leafs. The Islanders had lost the first two in Toronto. Then they'd won Game 3 (at The Coliseum) and Game 4 was the one that culminated in Shawn Bates' penalty-shot, when I thought the roof was going to come off The Coliseum. Man, I got chills doing that whole game. It was fabulous."

But before we get to Bates, Rose and their magical moment, let's set the stage.

The Eastern Conference Quarter-Finals series between the Maple Leafs and Islanders was the first time the Isles had been in the playoffs since being swept by the Rangers in 1994. It was and is the longest playoff drought in franchise history. So, it had been quite a long time for the Long Island fans since they'd had a chance to let loose and show why The Coliseum was essentially the "Sixth Man" on the ice for the Islanders.

ROSE: "The intensity (of that series), I mean it was just such an enormous battle. A battle for space. A battle for the puck. A battle in every facet of hockey. When you love the sport, you just relish games like that, because they're everything that hockey is.

"I was anxious and excited, because it was shaping up to be a really good series. And I was just so excited about the atmosphere in that building. I told guys who played for The Cup teams this and most of them thought I was crazy. Mike Bossy thought I was nuts when I said this to him. But, I would, to this day, submit that, that building, in those three games they played against Toronto in 2002, decibel-for-decimal, was probably louder than during The Cup years. It was just a different world by the early-2000's than it was in the early-1980's and people were just that much more demonstrative and loud.

"And you had the pent up excitement of being in the playoffs after so many years out. Plus, by 2002 it had been nearly 20-years since the last Cup year. So, the fans who remember the Cup seasons, they were a little hungry and the ones who didn't were overjoyed at getting their first taste.

"So, I really think that, that building was louder in '02, than it had been during The Cup years.

"(As for Game 4) it was an intense, intense game, which was made even more intense by the emotions of the crowd. You really feed off of that kind of energy, I would imagine players do as well. And I know the announcers do, because I do."

Well, that intensity and energy were on display early on as the Isles' Alexei Yashin and Toronto's Alexander Mogilny scored 9:14 apart in the first period, thus providing some early fireworks for both sides. (Mogilny's was a power-play goal).

And by comparison, the second period seemed somewhat tame as only one-goal was scored. But what a goal it was, as Tomas Kaberle scored with just 41-seconds to go in the period to give Toronto a 2-1 lead going into the final 20-minutes of the game. It was, or rather, it could have been a death-kneel to the Isles and their hopes of winning.

But it is a testament to the Islanders and their fans that they managed to rise above and fight back. It started at the 13:16 mark of the third period as Kip Miller recorded his own power-play goal to tie the game. And then 1:40 later, the Isles kept it going as Roman Hamrlik scored his first of the series to give Long Island its first lead of the game.

However, less than two-minutes after Hamrlik's goal, Toronto's big agitator, Shayne Corson, netted a goal of his own to once more tie the game. And just as overtime looked more and more likely, the Isles' Shawn Bates broke in behind the Leafs defense and was taken down from behind.

Here's where I'll let Rose take over.

ROSE: "There was some controversy over whether or not the play that resulted in the penalty-shot warranted one. But it did.

"As I recall, there was not unanimity of opinion that Bates had been clearly ahead of the pack and that he was pulled down from behind rather than the side. I mean, there are certain criteria for penalty-shots, which might or might not have been met depending on your point of view.

"I just remember that when the referee put his arm up for a penalty, what happens is, when the referee calls a penalty-shot, as the play evolves and continues, the first thing you see is that arm go up. And then, when, in this case, the Maple Leafs got control of the puck, the first thing I did was look to see if I had any suspicion that it could be a penalty-shot, whether the referee points to center ice or not. And he did.

"If I remember right, it was somewhat dramatic too. There was a split second when he blew the whistle. I don't remember who the referee was, but then he pointed to center ice and confirmed it would be a penalty-shot.

"What I remember, from my perspective, was Joe (Micheletti) analyzing the play that resulted in the penalty-shot and then beginning to set it up. And I don't know this, but maybe Joe speculated what Bates was going to do: deke, shoot, whatever his plan was.

"And I seem to remember Bates going to the bench before the penalty-shot and Michael Peca saying something to him, probably about what the best way to beat Curtis Joseph one-on-one would be.

"So anyway, what I recall was Joe finishing up his analysis and me wanting to say something to set up the inevitable shot. And I don't know if I was, or wasn't, waiting for Eric Hornick to show me, on the dry erase board, what number penalty-shot in Islanders playoff history this was going to be.

"And I remember that I almost talked over Bates making his move. I really wanted to leave a little more room at the beginning, when Bates took the puck at the red line. So, I remember I had to kind of rush what I was saying to stay on the shot. And then there was no call really, it was just, 'Bates in on goal, he shoots, scores!' and then just shut up and let the crowd carry it.

"I don't remember if I instinctively knew how long to give it before I talked or if I waited for our Producer to tell me when it was okay to talk. We all know in television that when you get a moment like that, you just shut up and let the crowd carry it.

"And what I do remember saying after that was something along the lines of, 'for a franchise that's had as many memorable post-season moments as the Islanders have, you've just seen one of the most memorable,' or words to that effect."

That memorable moment gave the Isles the win in Game 4, tied the series at two-games apiece AND ensured that Bates and Rose would be forever linked in Islanders history.

A PICTURE IS WORTH 1,000 WORDS

ROSE: "Well, on the ice it would clearly be the Bates penalty-shot, but, there's another one for me that I felt was my seal of approval from the Islanders fans. It was a little rocky the first couple of years, coming over from the Rangers. And remember how things were, the Rangers had just won The Cup a year-and-a-half before and I had been the Rangers announcer. Everybody knew, because I did a talk show in New York, that I'd grown up a Rangers fan.

"They didn't know I had a background with the Islanders that dated back to the very beginning. Those first few years, it was so bad and the fans were so angry about the state of the franchise and ownership and all that. I was caught right in the middle of it and I was one of the things that a lot of them didn't like. But, eventually I think they got comfortable with me and I started to win them over.

"Whenever there had been an on-ice ceremony my first few years with the Islanders, for whatever reason, I was not asked to emcee them. And I think internally there was a little, feeling among the Islanders hierarchy that I might get booed. It might be uncomfortable and that I should just do the radio. But then, late in the 2001-02 season, it all comes back to that year for me, the Islanders finally reached an agreement with Bryan Trottier that they were going to retire Bryan's number. And I'd known Bryan for a long-time.

"I considered him a friend and I said to whoever was running it, 'look, it's been six-years, I want to do this one. I think Bryan would be good with it, I'm ready to do it and I don't care what the reaction is, but I want to do this with Bryan. I want to emcee the ceremonies for Bryan because I'm that fond of him.' They said, 'sure, go ahead.' And I remember, I was a little apprehensive about what the crowd reaction would be, but, I was told I should be at the microphone when I'm introduced, not walking up to the microphone from the runway.

"I guess that was preemptive in case there was some booing; that I could jump right on it. So, the PA announcer introduced me and I was just overwhelmed by how positive the ovation was. I mean, it was a really, really nice, warm, welcoming ovation. And that was the moment I felt I'd arrived as an Islanders announcer. And I savor that memory."

18 NEIL SMITH (ISLANDERS SCOUT)
ISLES SURVIVE FIRST-ROUND SCARE FROM PENGUINS IN
QUEST FOR THREE-PEAT (@NASSAU COLISEUM)
APRIL 13, 1982
NYI 4, PIT 3 (OT)

BACKGROUND

If you are a hockey fan, there is a good chance you know who Neil Smith is. And if you are a fan of hockey in New York City -- and are at least high school aged -- then you definitely know who Neil Smith is.

For close to the last 40-years, Smith has been a mainstay in NHL circles as an executive and sometimes broadcaster. And although his track record of trades and free agent signings is open to debate, there is no doubting his ability to help build a winner.

Many fans will rightly point to Smith as the architect of the only Rangers Cup-championship in the last 80-years -- 1994. But there are many who seem to forget that he ALSO played a contributing role in TWO Cup-championships on Long Island during the heart of the Islanders dynasty.

From the start of the 1980-81 season to the end of the 1981-82 season, Smith served diligently as the Islanders Pro-Scout; often delivering packed reports to Isles Head Coach, Al Arbour. In fact, you can trace any success he had in his career back to his days with the Islanders, when he learned from the late, great Bill Torrey and from chief scout, Jimmy Devellano, who, as of this writing, is currently serving as the Senior Vice President/Alternate Governor of the Detroit Red Wings.

It's really quite the story to behold. So, without further ado, here it is.

SMITH: "I worked for them, back in 1981, when I suggested to them that I could go to all the games and pre-scout the other teams and no one would really know who I was. And that all came off of an incident that happened at Madison Square Garden one night when I was there. Lorne Henning, the Isles Assistant Coach, got into a big thing with a fan in the Blue Seats.

"And I realized that they (the Isles executives) could hardly even go in the building because of the rivalry. So, I could go into the building and they wouldn't know who I am and I could scout all the teams. I did it for free for the Islanders for the 1980-81 season and then in '81-'82, they hired me full-time to do that. That was my start.

"I was doing pro-scouting and I was going everywhere. I wasn't just going to The Garden. After Al Arbour saw how I was working he had me go everywhere. It was the start of something really good for me.

"I wanted to be in hockey. I loved hockey. I'd always played hockey and wanted to stay involved in it after I finished playing my little bit of pro that I played. I just tried to find a way to be involved and back then I was lucky enough that I was able to get that."

MOST UNFORGETTABLE ISLANDERS GAME

When the 1981-82 season started, the Islanders were two-time defending Stanley Cup champions and they were seeking to prove they truly were a dynasty by making it three-straight. But in order to get there they would have to qualify for the playoffs -- they did -- and make it through the grueling tournament that is the Stanley Cup Playoffs.

And as luck would have it, they drew a match-up with the Penguins in the first-round. Having won The League with 118-points this looked like a mismatch on paper; especially when you realize Pittsburgh only accumulated 75-points during the regular-season.

But there's a reason games aren't played on paper.

After trouncing the Penguins by a combined score of 15-3 in Games 1 and 2 at Nassau coliseum, the series shifted to Pittsburgh with the Isles eyeing an easy sweep. However, the Penguins weren't willing to let that happen and brought the Isles momentum to a screeching halt by winning Games 3 and 4 to force a "winner-take-all" Game 5 back at The Old Barn.

SMITH: "Pittsburgh had the Islanders at two-games a piece going back to Long Island and it really scared the heck out of you, because if they (the Islanders) had lost Game 5, their Cup-run was over.

"They (the Penguins) weren't a dominant team in The League by any stretch and that's why the Islanders played them in the first-round, because the Islanders that year, I believe, had won The League and came in first-overall. Pittsburgh was Number 8 in the Prince of Wales Conference and back in those days, Number 1 got to play Number 8.

"So it didn't look like they were going to be a formidable opponent coming in to play against the Islanders. They had some real good players. Randy Carlyle was a defenseman for them and he'd won the Norris Trophy one year. He was a pretty good defenseman. They had Mike Bullard, who was a pretty good goal-scorer. They had some real talent there, but they didn't have a really well oiled machine like the Islanders did. So, I don't think anybody was expecting the Penguins to come close to the Islanders that year.

"But they played a real physical brand against the Islanders and I think probably what happened was the team took the Penguins a little bit too lightly and maybe weren't prepared to get the opponent that it got."

When the game started neither team was able to gain an early advantage on the scoreboard, but there was a real sense of unease in The Coliseum, as everybody from the fans, the players, the media, etc. all hoped and prayed the Isles run would continue.

And then, at the 10:18 mark of the second period, Bobby Nystrom answered those prayers by putting the Islanders up 1-0 with just under half the game to go. Surely the team would add on to its lead and advance to the next round?

NOT. SO. FAST.

Less than a minute after Nystrom scored, Kevin McClelland got the Penguins on the board, tying the game at 1.

And then came the barrage that left the Isles reeling. Two more quick goals by the Penguins, one each from Bullard and Carlyle, gave Pittsburgh a 3-1 lead going into the third period. And to make matters worse, the Islanders went more than 14-minutes without scoring, meaning they were quite possibly in the final six-minutes of their season.

But if there was one thing the Islanders had learned during all of their playoff runs, it was that the game wasn't over until the final horn sounded. With 5:27 left, Mike McEwen netted a power-play goal to bring the Isles within 3-2 and, more importantly, bring the subdued crowd to life.

However, it was going to take more than one-goal to save the Islanders season. And that's when John Tonelli stepped up and delivered one of the biggest goals of his career. With just 2:21 remaining in regulation time, Tonelli beat Penguins goalie Michel Dion to tie the game and send the game to overtime.

The Islanders had staved off elimination, but the job wasn't done -- yet. Could they muster the willpower necessary to finish off the pesky Penguins?

The answer: Yes.

SMITH: "On the winning goal a couple of players, I think it was Tonelli and one of their defensemen tumbled into the boards and Tonelli got up quicker than their guy did, brought the puck back out to the front of the net and scored. And as I said, that was in overtime. When you get to overtime, it doesn't matter who was what seed, the next team to score is going to win the series. And so, that's why it was excruciating for the team and for the fans at The Coliseum. But I'll never forget Tonelli scoring that goal. It was amazing."

Finally, the Penguins had been vanquished and the Islanders were moving on with their eyes firmly focused on a third-straight Cup. And after rising to the challenge in the opening-round, they semi-coasted the rest of the way, having gained valuable experience from the adversity they faced against Pittsburgh.

A PICTURE IS WORTH 1,000 WORDS

SMITH: "I would say that it would be one of two things. It would either be sitting at Burger King with Al Arbour, while he was showing me these forms I had to fill out to be a pro-scout and thinking to myself, 'I was playing last year in the minors and now I'm with Al Arbour who's a Stanley Cup coach. He'd won The Cup the year before.

"And then, the other thing would probably be, after they beat Minnesota, the guys wanted me to come into the locker room. So I went in and they had me drinking out of the Stanley Cup and holding the Stanley Cup. It didn't seem like it could possibly be real. I mean, I had gone from a struggling minor league player to holding the Stanley Cup and being part of that. Even though it was a small part, I was still part of it. Those moments, in my mind's eye, are incredible."

19 ARTHUR STAPLE (NEWSDAY)
GAME 3: 2013 EASTERN CONFERENCE QUARTER-FINALS
(@NASSAU COLISEUM)
MAY 5, 2013
NYI 4, PIT 5 (OT)

BACKGROUND

When it comes to the relationship between writers and fans almost every fan has a particular writer or two who they prefer to read over everyone else. It's just the way things are.

And while most of the writers who cover your favorite teams are indeed friends -- or at least friendly with each other -- there is still competition over readership.

In New York, this is especially prevalent, as the number of publications and therefore writers, who cover your favorite teams have shrunk over the past decade. And this is particularly true in hockey.

But fear not, for there are still a number of hockey writers who have become so ingrained in the fabric of the team they cover that fans can't wait to open the newspaper or go online to read their latest articles.

And when it comes to the Islanders, nobody is more sought after for their coverage of the team than Arthur Staple, who currently is one of the senior most writers around the team on a daily basis. (And when I say senior, I mean in terms of consecutive years covering the team, not in age).

So, how did Arthur Staple get to where he is today?

STAPLE: "I first got interested in following sports when I was a kid. I grew up pretty close to Madison Square Garden and my older brother was a big Rangers fan, so we went to a few games and we'd watch a lot of games on TV. And then, I kind of got the bug that way.

"When I was in high school, at my school, we had an internship program when you were a senior and one of the internships that was listed was working with Stan Fischler. I had a bunch of his books from when I was a kid and I was pretty excited about it.

"So, I applied for the internship and got it. I spent a lot of time working with Stan and being his Rangers correspondent that season (1988-89). It was a pretty special experience to be 17-years-old and going into the Rangers locker room, interviewing players and trying to act like a professional sports writer.

"Then, I went off to college at Boston University, where I studied journalism and kind of learned a little bit more about the ropes (of being a sports writer).

"I interned at *The Daily News* when I just got out of college and I thought that would kind of be my springboard to staying there full-time, but that wasn't really a possibility. So, I freelanced for a couple of places in the Tri-State area, including *The Bergen Record* in New Jersey. That was around the time the Rangers won the Stanley Cup in '94.

"Then, after I did some other freelance work. My first full-time job was in 1997, at the *Stamford Advocate* up in Connecticut. I was there for six-months and then an opening came up at *Newsday* and they hired me back. I ended up working as a part-timer at *Newsday* in their city office, covering high school sports, college sports and working my way up.

"My first season covering the Rangers (for *Newsday*) was 2001-02 and I did that until the full-year lockout in 2004-05. I covered the NFL after that and then, in 2011-12, I was back covering the Islanders.

"Then, in 2018, I switched publications from *Newsday* to *The Athletic*, but I still continue to cover the Islanders. So, I'm in year-nine right now with the Islanders."

MOST UNFORGETTABLE ISLANDERS GAME

The 2012-13 NHL season was a strange one for sure. Due to a lockout, the season didn't start until January and it was condensed from

82-games down to 48-games. And due to the severe reduction in games, the importance on gathering points was amplified beyond belief, for any sort of bad start would likely derail any chance a team had at making the playoffs. So, what did the Islanders do?

STAPLE: "They (the Islanders) started off really poorly that year. I think there were like 4-7-1 or something. So it looked a lot like a couple of years before that, when they were sort of out of it by Thanksgiving. Obviously, it was different because the schedule was so condensed and we are starting in January instead of October, but they were having the same kind of struggles and Evgeni Nabokov was really kind of the key to all of it.

"He was the guy who had been around a lot. That was his second-year, I think, with them and they didn't really have a backup goalie to speak of that year. Kevin Poulin was really the guy who was kind of a nominal backup. So, Nabby had to play a ton and I think they only lost once in regulation in their last 15 or 16 regular-season games.

"They just kept getting points any way they could, even with overtime or shootout losses. They just kind of grabbed onto a playoff spot at some point and held on. And I think, they gave away a couple of points at the end of the regular-season that would have had them in maybe a better spot, they probably would've played Washington, maybe, instead of the Penguins, which seemed, at the time, like an easier match-up.

"So, the fact that they got in was definitely a surprise and I think nobody really thought that they could do more than maybe win a game against Pittsburgh. But it turned out to be a lot more competitive than that.

"A couple of years before, there was the crazy fight night at The Coliseum, in February of 2011, when the Islanders went out and won the game very decisively. And also, they had most of their team ejected throughout the course of the game.

"I think there were maybe 15 guys left on the bench on both sides. Michael Haley had gotten called up because of that game. They also had Trevor Gillies. It all stemmed from a couple of incidents in a game about a week before in Pittsburgh when Max Talbot hit Blake Comeau with kind of a borderline hit and he ended up with a concussion. And then, the more famous one was Brent Johnson fighting Rick DiPietro and delivering the one-punch knockout that pretty much ended DiPietro's season with multiple facial fractures.

"The Islanders were definitely always the underdog and always kind of punching up, so to speak, against the Penguins. And, I think that, that night, from two-years before kind of solidified this, as the Islanders were a team who hadn't made the playoffs in like the past six- or seven-seasons. So, if they had any sort of rival, it was the Penguins. And that was the team they most wanted to beat, because the Penguins had been beating up on them, literally and figuratively, for a long time.

"It (the series) was 1-1 and the first game in Pittsburgh was a total no-show for the Islanders. The Penguins were a couple of years removed from winning the Stanley Cup. They had (Sidney) Crosby and (Evgeni) Malkin and the usual cast of characters. The Islanders were totally shell-shocked in that first game.

"And then, in the second game the Penguins were up, I think 2-0 or maybe 3-1 and Kyle Okposo fought Matt Niskanen and tuned him up pretty good. I think that kind of woke the Islanders up and Fleury gave up a couple of soft ones and they (The Islanders) won that Game 2. So, they came back 1-1 and it didn't seem quite as insurmountable.

"I think, even if it was 2-0 Pittsburgh, the Islanders fans who were there, they had waited so long for a playoff series and some sort of promising team. That was (John) Tavares' first playoff series. So it just sort of felt like they were starting to turn the corner a little bit. And of the three home games that series; there were a couple of overtime wins by the Penguins. The Islanders won the other one.

"(And) the funny thing, for me, in that series, was it was already May, but it felt a lot later. And Jack Capuano, who was the Islanders' coach at the time, was a very, very superstitious guy. So, while we were on the road that year, I think I covered pretty much every road game. There were seasons at *Newsday* where I kind of ducked out on a few road trips to keep my family sane and keep myself sane. But, that year, because we hadn't really done anything for the first-half of the year, I was kind of expected to do all the games and it was very condensed and there was a lot of stress and anxiety with all the traveling around; especially in such a short space of time and especially that winter.

"So, by the time the playoffs rolled around, I was a little bit worn out. Jack had gotten used to a group of us: the coaches, Garth Snow the GM, a couple of PR people and I was included in that group because I was really the only beat writer. We would almost always find a place, a gym in some cities to play basketball, either between the morning skate and the game or preferably on an off-day.

"So I remember the off-day between Games 1 and 2 and they lost, I think it was 5-0 in Game 1. That off-day I got a text from the PR guy saying to meet them at this place and he sent me the address. It was like a health club in downtown Pittsburgh that had a pretty nice basketball court, which we had played on a couple of years before, or at least, a year before. And everybody got a good sweat.

"It was a lot of middle-aged guys, some of whom had been pro athletes, but not in basketball, just kind of working out the kinks, yelling at each other and getting physical. And then they turned around and won Game 2. So, we came home, we didn't play basketball back here, but I just remember coming home from that and I was a little bit banged up I guess from getting bounced around by guys like Brent Thompson and Doug Weight and Jack and Garth especially, because Garth is a load on the basketball court.

"So, I had a day to recover on the off-day between Games 2 and 3. But that noon start for Game 3 meant that I was getting up early and getting out there early. So, I was just kind of feeling like it had been a long season and now I was physically getting banged around. Maybe it was meant to feel like the way the players were feeling in that playoff series and just to suck it up and get through to the end.

"That Game 3, it was the loudest I'd heard it (The Coliseum) in a long time. And that series was such a strange one, because Evgeni Nabokov didn't make a ton of saves for the Islanders in that series, but Marc-Andre Fleury, I think people forget that the Penguins pulled him in favor of Tomas Vokoun, because he couldn't stop any shots. I think the Islanders scored a couple of quick goals in Game 3 and the place was ready to explode.

"It was really something. The place was always loud when there were more than 10,000 people in it. But that was when it was full to capacity and the fans hadn't seen a playoff game in so long. They were pretty much ready to jump through the roof.

"I think, to a lot of people and kind of a lot of us sitting in the press box and it's very close quarters in the press box at The Coliseum, so you can usually hear people just fine. But (that day) it looked like a silent movie because it was just so loud and everything felt like it was moving. And that was from the minute that they opened the doors at like 10:00 AM or 10:30, or whatever it was. Those NBC games start a little bit after the hour, so it's a bit different timing from a normal game.

"Normally, warm-ups start maybe a half-hour before the game. But this was getting closer to maybe 11:40 and from about 11:20 on, they (the fans) just kept going with 'Let's Go Islanders,' chants. They were stomping. They were loud. It was crazy.

"The Islanders jumped out to a lead (thanks to goals by Matt Moulson and Casey Cizikas). I think the two-goals came in the first five-and-a-half minutes of that game. And there were some pretty big (momentum) swings in that one. I think they (the Islanders) rode the adrenaline and some very bad goaltending from Fleury to that early lead. So it sort of felt like, 'maybe this isn't going to last.'

"Then the Penguins kind of gathered themselves and got a 5-on-3 late in the first period and converted both ends of it to tie the game. And that slowed some people down. It sort of felt like, 'all right, this is probably how it's supposed to go.' They (the Penguins) then ended up taking a lead at the end of that first period and then a two-goal lead into the third.

"The Islanders ended up having a rally from two-goals down to get to overtime. It was just nonstop. It was (Kyle) Okposo who got a short-handed goal to cut it back to a one-goal lead and I think that got everybody going. The goal by Okposo, I don't recall it being such a great shot. But Fleury just couldn't make a save. And that really gave the Islanders life. And then (John) Tavares scored his first goal of the series, his first ever playoff goal and that helped get it to overtime."

Unfortunately for the Islanders, that was the end of their feel-good comeback as a questionable call by the officials essentially handed the game to Pittsburgh.

STAPLE: "It was a kind of a weak penalty call against Brian Strait on Sidney Crosby, who drew the penalty, in overtime that led to another power-play goal, this one by Chris Kunitz who scored the winner. And I think that took the air out of the building a little bit. But I think also the fans felt like they didn't necessarily think that this was a series they could win.

"It was a very evenly played game too. Sometimes those overtimes can be a little bit lopsided. But the Islanders outshot them 36-25 in that game. Really, the power-play was the thing that ended up making the difference in that game. The Islanders just could not stop the Penguins' power-play. I think losing that game hurt, but I also feel they felt it was kind of a weak call for an overtime in a playoff game. They also seemed to feel afterwards that they hadn't just stolen a game in Pittsburgh (in Game 2). They weren't ready to go quietly (in that series).

"And I remember Brian Strait, after the game, with his very heavy Boston accent, saying that it was bullsh*t that he got called for that penalty."

While the call was almost definitely the wrong one, the Islanders had still shown they were a capable team and that one game would not define them. So, while they did not win the game or the series, it did help lay the foundation for the future playoff series' that were still to come.

A PICTURE IS WORTH 1,000 WORDS

STAPLE: "The biggest moment I remember the most is probably the (John) Tavares series-winning goal against the Panthers in 2016. As I mentioned before, when you're watching in overtime, especially double-overtime of a night game, you're usually watching it on TV and the TVs in the pressroom at Barclays Center are on a bit of a delay. But there is a game clock in the pressroom.

"So, when you're watching the TV, you're also watching the clock and then the clock stops and you think something interesting might be coming. And for that one, the clock stopped and you could sort of hear the fans.

"I mean, it's a really well built arena because you don't really get a lot of noise from outside that room, but when that clock stopped, the puck was down in the Islanders' end and I thought, 'uh-oh, did they lose this? Are we going back to Florida for Game 7?' And then I watched the rush up the ice and saw the guys' reactions, jumping up and down. I've seen that clip a lot over the years.

"And I think people like to, obviously people not from around here, like to rag on the Islanders. I certainly rag on them sometimes too, because it's the team I cover. But in nine-years, and this year they're going to head to their fifth playoffs in those nine, all things considered in recent Islanders' history, that's not too bad. I feel like there's more positives than negatives and that's probably the most positive one we've seen so far."

20 JOHN STERLING (WMCA/WGBB/WGLI)
UNLIKELY HERO PROPELS ISLES TO GAME 5 WIN OVER
SABRES
(@BUFFALO MEMORIAL AUDITORIUM)
APRIL 20, 1976
NYI 4, BUF 3

BACKGROUND

As a sports fan, when you think of John Sterling you immediately picture one of his joyous "YANKEES WIN! TTTHHHEEE YANKEES WIN!" calls. But for fans of a different generation, Sterling's unique blend of enthusiasm and keen sense, invokes a different picture; one from before he ever entered the both at Yankee Stadium.

Of course, I'm talking about the days when Sterling was the radio voice of the Islanders. What's that you say? You're wondering when John Sterling called Islanders games? Well, Sterling actually predates -- not by much -- the Islanders dynasty.

You see, Sterling was the soundtrack of the Islanders rise to power from 1975-1978; a time when the Islanders were just beginning to find themselves as a team, although not quite ready to rule The League. And it was during this time that Sterling created his beloved, "Goal! ISLANDER GOAL!" call that was often repeated back at him by the fans and even by then Isles G.M. Bill Torrey.

But how did Sterling, who admitted that from an early age he knew he was going to be on air, get to be in such a coveted position?

Well John, take it away.

STERLING: "Well, it's pretty easy of how I got into it. When I was 10-years-old, I'm just using 10 as a number. If you said to me, 'Do you really remember that?' Of course not, but I knew I was going to be on the air when I was that young. I never had to worry. I was going to be on the air. I did this because I love it. In my life, I do things I love and I totally ignore things I don't love. So, I listened to every radio and TV station.

"I wanted to be a disc jockey. I listened to the disc jockeys on the different stations. WNEW was my favorite by far. I thought that was the end of the world. I listened to every sportscaster, to music, to movies and Broadway shows. I was a fountain of knowledge at that time. I got on the air as a boy disc jockey.

"And then I got my first market a couple of years later in Providence and I was playing rock; although, then it was really kind of bubblegum rock. Anyway, I did that for a couple of years and then I got a great break. I was a staff announcer at WPAT and I got a great break one summer. The all-night guy needed hernia surgery, so, the program director had heard my tape and he said, 'I'll give you the month this guy's going to be out and if you're any good, then you can fill-in for anyone who goes on vacation.'

"So, I was there all summer long. It was a great thing for me to do. And at the same time, I contacted an agent through someone else and this gal gave me a chance to interview for a new talk show that Metro Media was starting. They had just bought a station in Baltimore and they wanted to have a show that was kind of like the show that a guy named Joe Pyne did in LA.

"That was a big break in my life. I had a big-time, general talk show -- not sports -- but I kept putting sports in it and before long I started getting some games and that led to WMCA, which was a sports talk show. And there I did a lot of games.

"So then I was doing Morgan State football and I talked to my program director about getting the new WHA team (World Hockey Association) that was going to start playing that fall. He said, 'go make a deal.'

"That could never happen today. Never. I wanted to do hockey. I had never done hockey and I loved it since I was a little boy going to Rangers games. So I made a deal with them, like a 50-50 deal and they were happy to do it. So now I had a chance to do hockey. I was doing football at Morgan State and hockey with the New York Raiders and then that led to the Nets and Islanders.

"So that's how I got to be able to broadcast all these sports. And as far as the Islanders, it really helped that I had the Raiders.

"Hockey is a very quick rhythm and you have to get that rhythm down; which I did. I loved doing the Islanders. We did all the home games and a lot of the road games. I was doing, with the Nets and the Islanders, about 125 games a year; including the talk show at WMCA.

"It was a lot, but I loved every minute. Now the Islanders were good when I got there. They hadn't won yet, but they were now going to the Semi-Finals and they used to sell out at home; they won an awful lot of home games. So it was a great job."

MOST UNFORGETTABLE ISLANDERS GAME

For the first two-years of the Islanders existence the team was nowhere near competitive. But that all changed during the 1974-75 season as they made the playoffs for the first time in franchise history; thus kick starting a run of 14-consecutive years making the playoffs.

And it was during the '74-'75 playoff year that the Islanders began to craft an identity of dramatic, late-game comebacks in the post-season that would be their trademark for over a decade. An 0-3 hole against Pittsburgh in the second-round became an Islanders series victory after becoming only the second team in NHL history to comeback from down 0-3 to win the series in seven-games.

They also came close to replicating the feat in the following round when they were down 0-3 to the Flyers and came back to force a Game 7, before ultimately falling victim to Philadelphia. But those experiences proved crucial the following year as the Islanders once again found themselves in need of a furious, slightly miraculous comeback.

The 1975-76 season was an impressive one for the Boys of Long Island as they topped the 100-point plateau for the first time in franchise history. And they also qualified for the playoffs for the second-straight year. Two quick wins over the Vancouver Canucks in the opening-round gave the Isles a world of momentum as they headed into their second-round match-up with the Buffalo Sabres.

However, two quick defeats up in Buffalo at the hand of the Sabres left the Islanders reeling and in need of another miracle -- albeit not as much of a miracle as they needed against Pittsburgh and Philadelphia the year prior -- if they wanted to keep their Stanley Cup dreams alive.

And that's precisely what Long Island got as the doctor prescribed a trip back to Nassau Coliseum for Games 3 and 4, where the Islanders rediscovered their mojo by winning both games to tie the series at two-games apiece.

Then it was back to Buffalo for a critical Game 5. If the Islanders could pull off a third-straight win then they would have a chance to close out the series at home a couple nights later in Game 6. But should they fail, then they would be forced to play Game 6 with their backs against the wall and the threat of their impressive season being washed away far too soon.

STERLING: "Game 5 happened when I had one of the greatest broadcasting weeks of my life in the late-70's. The Nets made the playoffs and they were playing San Antonio. And the Islanders were in the playoffs playing against Buffalo. When you put the two cities together, Buffalo and San Antonio, I was flying back-and-forth.

"The Islanders were down to Buffalo 0-2 and they won the next two games on the Island and the fifth game was in Buffalo."

And that fifth game did not start well for the visitors as Buffalo grabbed an early 2-0 lead thanks to goals by Richard Martin and Danny Gare within the first 6:57 of the first period. But the Isles were not willing to concede defeat. All they needed was one-goal to get back in the game. And that's exactly what they got as Andre St. Laurent scored just 43-seconds after Gare to pull the Islanders within 2-1.

All of a sudden this was a game again. No longer was there a threat of a blowout. And six-and-a-half minutes later the game was tied as J.P. Parise scored on the power-play to ease any tension that might have been creeping into the minds of the Isles players.

From there the teams remained deadlocked at 2 as the remainder of the first and all of the second period went by without either side scoring a goal. But that would soon change in the third.

With just over half of the third period gone, Jim Lorentz put the puck past Billy Smith for the 3-2 Buffalo lead and once again forced the Isles to fight from underneath. Could the Islanders tie the game again? Or would they be flying home to The Coliseum praying to stave off elimination?

STERLING: "They were down by a goal with just a few minutes left. The puck was loose along the left boards and J.P. Parise, who was a tough guy, a terrific player, was battling two of the Sabres; battling, banging, scrapping.

"He finally got the puck and he flipped it back to Denis Potvin, who was in the upper slot and Denny popped in the one-timer. He hit it as hard as you can hit it and found an open spot over goalie Gerry Desjardins and that tied the game.

"Now there was under a minute to play and there was a face-off in the right face-off circle in the Buffalo end. The puck went back and was thrown across to the other wing and picking it up was Bert Marshall, the defenseman, who never scored.

"So everyone, if you could picture this, skated from right to left, to where the puck was and Bert Marshall floated a shot on goal. He didn't have a great shot and there was so much traffic in front of Desjardins that he didn't see it. It went in. and the Islanders won the game. I thought that was great."

Denis Potvin and Bert Marshall had come through when the team needed them most and now it was on to Game 6, not with their backs against the wall, but rather, with a chance to close out the series and advance to the next round.

A PICTURE IS WORTH 1,000 WORDS

STERLING: "Well, I think it would be the game I told you about, when the Islanders beat Buffalo in Buffalo. Buffalo had home-ice advantage and the Islanders were down 2-0 (in the series). Then, they (the Islanders) won two-games on the Island before winning Game 5 in Buffalo. And I think that was also the year I was going back and forth between the Nets and the Islanders in the playoffs. That was the most exciting week I've ever had. Wow, what a great week! The Nets wound up beating San Antonio, then they won The Title and then they moved into the NBA. Anyway, that game in Buffalo, Game 5, it was really exciting (and part of a fantastic week!)"

21 RICHARD TORREY (SON OF NY ISLANDERS GM BILL
TORREY)
ISLES KEEP THREE-PEAT DREAMS ALIVE AFTER FIRST-
ROUND SCARE VS. PITTSBURGH
(@NASSAU COLISEUM)
APRIL 13, 1982
NYI 4, PIT 3 (OT)

BACKGROUND

There's nothing quite like being able to say that your father was
the architect of one of the greatest teams in NHL history. But that's
exactly what Richard Torrey could say, seeing as his father was "Bow-
Tie" Bill Torrey.

And while many would likely sit back and take advantage of
that, Richard decided he wanted to be a part of the action as well. So,
when he graduated college he got a job with the Islanders. And it was a
role that was crucial to the team's success, for he was the Video
Statistician. (More on that later).

But Richard Torrey was and is much more than just his father's
son. Richard was a success in his own right. And with "Bow-Tie" Bill
having sadly passed on in May 2018, it is important to keep his stories
alive.

So, this chapter is a unique one, as you will hear stories from
Richard Torrey, both about his own time with the Islanders and also
about his father's time with the Islanders.

TORREY: "The winter before (the Islanders began play) it was Christmas time (in 1971). My dad (the late-Bill Torrey) had, up until the previous season, worked for the California Seals and he was fired, or we have now found a letter that he wrote to Charlie Finley, which says he was quitting and he gave him a big F-U in the letter.

"But, in any event, he was back in Pittsburgh. He had a promotional agency in the Civic Arena, which was kind of an offshoot from his years with the Pittsburgh Hornets. We (my dad, my brothers and I) were at dinner and he just all of a sudden said, 'I've got some opportunities to go back into hockey and I just wanted to run them by you.'

"He actually was offered the Atlanta job as well, but he didn't really expound on that one with us. What he said was, 'I'm thinking of taking a job on Long Island,' and my first thought was, 'Oh great, he's going back to California.' I had no idea where Long Island was. I must've thought it was Long Beach or something. (To clarify) I was born in LA. (My brothers were born all over the place). But my parents were divorced when I was five, so we would spend our school year in Pittsburgh with our mom and all holidays, summers and extra time with our dad.

"So, we spent a lot of time out in California. At the time it really wasn't hockey country, at least not in Oakland. But, when he came back to Pittsburgh we kind of thought, 'okay good, we'll be seeing you a lot more.' So when he said, 'It's up to you guys,' at the time I was 11 and to me it was a no brainer. I said, 'you have to, it's your passion.'

"Anyway, that summer in 1972, we were looking for houses on Long Island and after moving there, we'd go to his office -- the original Islanders' offices -- which was on the second floor of the Marine Midland Bank on Old Country Road; at least, that's where I think it was. But it was a one-room operation. One room. It was because it was in the New York Nets' offices. We'd walk through the Nets' offices and then in the back was one office, with a secretary outside. And then there was my dad's office and there was a crayon drawing of the Islanders' logo on the wall, which Roy Boe's wife had designed and drawn."

From there, Richard Torrey continued to be a presence around the team as his dad, (the late-Bill Torrey) always made sure his sons (all four of them) were well indoctrinated in the "Islanders Way." And once Richard Torrey graduated college in the early 1980's, he went to work in the "family business."

TORREY: "I graduated from college in '81 and I went immediately into running or helping to run the Islander hockey school with Neil Smith. We shared an office. That was the first thing I did. I was doing that because I had played and they needed someone to run the hockey school. So Neil and I took that up and it was during that summer that Al Arbour's son, Jay, had gotten a job. So, now someone was needed to do the videotaping of all the games and then to break the games down afterwards into power-play, penalty-kill, etc. There were certain players to watch. Tapes had to be made. It was all-dependent on who the team was playing against and whether it was a good team or whatever.

"Then you would set up a deck or a cassette player in either the locker room or right to the side of the locker room so that Al could come in between periods or whatever. He might have wanted to see something, so you had to have the stuff ready. He was an early video guy. In fact, he actually had his wife Claire operating a reel-to-reel. Then he had his son do it. And then I did it.

"He was kind of a pioneer in analytics. But when I did it I had an old accounting ledger and I kept all the stats he wanted me to keep on the entire team and then I'd break that down. So, I guess my title was Video Statistician and I did that from the year we beat Vancouver -- '82-'83 -- through the year we lost to Edmonton -- '83-'84."

MOST UNFORGETTABLE ISLANDERS GAME

By 1982 the Islanders had won two-straight Cups and were seeking the one thing that could and would solidify them as a dynasty; a third-consecutive Stanley Cup. And when the 1981-82 regular-season was over, the Islanders sat atop the Patrick Division standings with an astounding 118-points.

It seemed like all the pieces were in place for a smooth ride through the playoffs, but a speed bump named Pittsburgh reared its head in the Division Semi-Finals. With the first two games at Nassau Coliseum, the Isles trounced the Penguins 8-1 and 7-2 to take a commanding 2-0 series lead. And in those days, the Division Semi-Finals were just a best-three-of-five. So, the Islanders needed just one more win to advance to the next round.

However, that one win would be hard to come by.

TORREY: "Back then the first-round of the playoffs was a best-three-of-five series. And we (the Islanders) won the first two games. Then we flew to Pittsburgh and we checked into the Chatham Center Hotel. Game 3 was the following day. And this was right around Easter.

"So, we were up two-games-to-one and we already have two Cups under our belt. We went to The Civic Arena and we had already checked out of the hotel. The Penguins found out and put that on their bulletin board. They felt we were pretty cocky. That we already had the game won and the game hadn't even started yet.

"And, of course, the Islanders lost that game. So, we had to go back to the Chatham Center and check back in. Nobody had eaten. It was Easter Sunday and there was nothing open. I remember this one guy, Tom Barnwell, 'Tom The Bomb,' he was able to find stuff. He found a pizza place and got like 40 pizzas so the team could eat.

"Then we had the next game there the following night and we lost that game too. So, then we headed back to Long Island for Game 5.

"Since it was in the playoffs, I probably had already gone to Al's house the night before and either sat with him as he looked at videotape for awhile or at least set him up so he could watch tapes all night and chain smoke. Chain-smoke and drink coffee in this tiny little office in his basement until like 3 or 4 o'clock in the morning.

"Then, the following morning I would have talked to him or to Lorne Henning, who was the Assistant Coach to see if I was supposed to run the machines during the game. So, if I remember correctly, I was probably running tapes to Lorne's house and maybe Al's that morning (of Game 5) and maybe getting requests for what I would need to break down.

"So I'd be doing video editing with really just a line of VCRs. I would then go to the game and get to The Coliseum around three or four in the afternoon. Again, depending on what Al's preference would be, I'd be setting up a machine in the room directly across from the Islanders' locker room or just be in my office. And then I'd be in game mode starting like an hour before the game.

"(Going into that game) I was nervous. I was very nervous, only because they had a hot goalie, Michel Dion and they had been taking it to us. I believe they won Game 3 in overtime in Pittsburgh. They had nothing to lose. They were playing with house money. They were loose. We were not. We were tight.

"It was like, 'we don't want this to end. We've just won two Cups. We can't let Pittsburgh beat us in the first-round of the playoffs.' So we were definitely tight and we played tight. Those first two periods we did not play Islanders' hockey. We were down 3-1 after the second period."

"Now, generally, I would be back in my office doing the videotaping in case Al (Arbour) wanted anything from me. He would have told me before the game if there was anything he would want to look at in between periods. So, I would be running that to the locker room and then running right back and starting up again.

"But during the third period I was losing my mind. I just let the tape run and I went out and watched it. It was such a blur. It was as close to having the dynasty end at two (Cups) as I could ever remember; other then when we finally lost it."

When the third period began it really looked like the Islanders were out of gas and that their run was all but over. However, to a man, each player on the roster upped his game and resumed playing the game the way they knew they were capable of.

It started with Mike McEwen scoring a power-play goal at the 14:33 mark of the period to bring the Isles within a goal of tying the game. But as time continued to tick off the clock the prospect of another Isles victory seemed bleak. That is, until a hero emerged from the shadows. And that hero's name was John Tonelli.

With just 2:21 left in the third period, Gord Lane fired the puck into Pittsburgh's zone and it went off the boards behind Michel Dion's net. The puck bounced over the stick of Penguins' defenseman Randy Carlyle and right out to Tonelli who sniped it home to tie the game in dramatic fashion and necessitated overtime.

And with both teams' seasons hanging on by a thread -- such is the nature of a winner-take-all playoff game in overtime -- Tonelli again stepped up, this time delivering what is very likely the goal of his career, as he put home Bob Nystrom's rebound at the 6:19 mark of overtime to send the Isles to the Patrick Division Finals against the Rangers.

TORREY: "That game, in my mind, is one of the greatest Islanders games ever."

A PICTURE IS WORTH 1,000 WORDS

TORREY: "I have a different take on it now because of my dad's passing. But it's sitting on a team bus or a team flight and on the buses we're even closer together. I'd be in the second row and I'd be behind Al Arbour and my dad. It was hundreds of times that I did that. And in a sense, it was sort of a symbol of the fact that I was with them; going to a game or going to the airport or going wherever.

"What also stands out in my mind, being his (Bill Torrey's) son and all the guys behind us, all the knuckleheads doing things, or being totally silent because it was 2 o'clock in the morning and they had just landed in Toronto or wherever. But having those two at the helm and just sort of being an observer of that. My job, anyone could have done it really. But being there to see those two and what they accomplished, that would be the picture."

BONUS

REMEMBERING THE LATE-BILL TORREY

Bill Torrey was the architect of the Islanders from before they ever played a game in the NHL. And it was a post he proudly held from 1971 (the year before the Isles officially began play) until 1992.

Without the Late-Torrey, the Islanders as we currently know them would have never come to be.

So, in honor of the man who created the very culture of the Islanders, I caught up with one of his sons, Richard, to remind Islanders fans everywhere just how special "Bow-Tie" Bill was and how, while he may be gone, his legacy still endures to this day.

Here are some of the memories Richard Torrey shared about his dad.

R. TORREY: "Those two (Al Arbour and my dad, Bill Torrey) had the most remarkable working relationship I've ever seen. They were as close to being brothers as you could possibly get.

"To go out to dinner with those two on the road or whatever, it was magnificent. It was just, again, when you're that young, you're not thinking about it, but I wish I had had a tape recorder. I wish I wrote down some of the stuff because they would just start telling stories and stuff.

"There would be times when Al would need to be settled down and my dad could do it. My dad would joke with him. My dad would just pester him and kind of diffuse it. They were just such an awesome duo."

And in terms of his dad's favorite games, here are two stories that every Islanders fan should know about "Bow-Tie" Bill, as they show how truly remarkable he was.

R. TORREY: "After that first Cup victory against Philly, I'll never forget this as long as I live. First of all, his father, even while he was with the Islanders, was telling him, 'you need to get a real job. When are you going to get a real job?' He used to say to him all the time. And when my dad was working for the Pittsburgh Hornets, he was trying to get my dad to move back to Ottawa and go work for Lever Brothers Soap. He wanted him to go work for a soap company. So the big joke was, 'when are you going to get a real job?'

"And I'll never forget this. So, when my dad won his first Cup, he got the champagne bath and whatever and then he went back to his office and the first thing he did was call his dad. And with every Cup after that the first thing he would do was call his dad and say, 'fooled 'em again.'

"And when my dad went into the Hall of Fame, I remember he mentioned his dad asking him, 'when was he going to get a real job?' And I guess he never did.

"So that first Cup was big, because he could finally say to his dad, 'I got a real job.'

"But I also think, as important to him was winning that first playoff series, the one against the Rangers in 1975, because that's really when the Islanders became the Islanders in a way. Up until then they were 'Torrey's Turkeys.'

"At The Coliseum, people had taken construction paper and put it up on the glass spelling out, 'Torrey's Turkeys.' They were horrible. And it took three-years for them to get rid of that stigma and start out on a different path. That first series win against the Rangers did it."

And perhaps the final thing about the late-Bill Torrey is how much he always made sure to keep pushing forward.

R. TORREY: "It's fascinating to look at, but through all those years, my dad didn't wear his rings. He didn't do stuff like that, like resting on his laurels or anything. He always immediately started thinking about what was next and maybe that was part of his secret."

22 ED WESTFALL (NY ISLANDERS)
THE CAPTAIN COMES THROUGH IN THE CLUTCH!
(@PITTSBURGH CIVIC ARENA)
APRIL 26, 1975
NYI 1, PIT 0

BACKGROUND

Being the first to do something is usually a pretty good thing. And sometimes, it's even special.

When the Islanders began play in 1972, they were a rag-tag group of players who had been plucked from other teams, or drafted in the Amateur Draft. And some of those players who were selected from other NHL teams weren't necessarily going to be a long-term part of the Islanders plans.

But, one such player was a part of those plans and his name was Ed Westfall.

Westfall had been a member of the Bruins for 11-years before the Islanders made him the first player in franchise history; courtesy of the Expansion Draft. It was a shock to the system for sure for Westfall, but it was one that he ended up embracing.

In fact, he embraced it so much that G.M. Bill Torrey made him the first ever captain in team history. And what a captain he was!

It wasn't all milk and honey at first though. There was a lot of losing, as well as the constant threat of the World Hockey Association. There were even money issues. But nevertheless, Westfall remained true to the Islanders.

And it's thanks to Westfall's leadership that the Islanders were able to "grow up" so fast. By their third season the Islanders were making waves in the playoffs and Westfall was right in the thick of things. But how did this Bruin turned Islander end up in the NHL in the first place?

WESTFALL: "Well, I suppose the fact that kids growing up, specifically in Ontario, where I grew up, near Toronto and all over Canada, we all played hockey.

"We all dreamt about being an NHL player. So, it was a following your dreams kind of thing. As you progressed and went along, you got better and then they moved you up and they (teams) keep an eye on you. Back then there wasn't a draft. We belonged to a city, in this case, Oshawa, where I was. And any kid that had any kind promise out of Oshawa belonged to the Boston Bruins; it was like being a horse or a cow.

"So, anyway, as I said, things got better and I improved, along with a lot of other guys. It's a process of elimination. So then I got to Junior Hockey, which was the next big step. When you're a teenager, 16 to 20, which really kind of separated you from a whole lot of people, because you were moving up to a grade of hockey that's one step away from being professional. And if you can make it through that and continue to improve, then your chances of making it to the NHL are much better.

"I was in the sphere of the Toronto Maple Leafs, but most of us kids were Gordie Howe fans. And then, when you got to a certain point, you were watching, the junior team in your area. In my case, because I was in the sphere of the Boston Bruins and I knew if I got far enough that I'd be a Bruin, so we watched the Bruins; or at least I did. I wanted to know what they were doing.

"As a 16, 17-year-old, I got to go to Junior Hockey and I wore hand-me-down Bruin uniforms from the NHL team. So, you were inaugurated in a certain way as a junior. I played in a little town called Barrie Ontario, and it had a 'B' obviously. And the Bruins were from Boston, so they gave us their old sweaters; that's what we played in.

"My last year of junior I was 20, so by the next fall I was 21-years of age and I made the Bruins team. I spent 11-years with the Bruins, watching them go from the worst team in hockey to the best team in hockey. And then, when we won our second Stanley Cup in 1972, the Islanders and the original Atlanta Flames came into the NHL as new franchises. They had an Expansion Draft and the Islanders, I guess, in a toss, got the first pick and Bill Torrey picked me.

"I went from the best team in hockey to the worst in a matter of a few months. So anyway, it was a bit of a shock and a big setback, probably for my family more than me. But I ended up an Islander and at first I didn't know where Long Island was.

"Having played against the Rangers all those years, I knew where New York City was, but not Long Island. Anyway, I got to meet Bill Torrey and I got to meet some of the people who were running the team, like Roy Boe in particular. I was a big fan of Roy. He was trying like heck to make an NHL franchise work on Long Island. I bought in and a way we went."

Of course, things weren't exactly smooth sailing in the early going for the Islanders, but "Bow-Tie" Bill had an idea of who he wanted to help settle things down and how he wanted to do so. And that involved making Westfall the inaugural captain of the team.

WESTFALL: "It was kind of mundane. I never thought about it. All I was thinking about was trying to make this franchise better. 11 of the players who were drafted by the Islanders jumped to the World Hockey Association that first year and, of course, I was being asked to jump to the WHA as well.

"But as far as the captain thing goes, I never thought about it until Bill Torrey came up to me early on in Training Camp and said, 'I want you to be the captain of the team.' You don't say 'no' or that you don't want to. Back then it was quite an honor to be elected the captain of the team. And that's really how it came about. There were no horns or whistles or red carpets or anything like that. He asked if I'd take the captaincy and I said, 'yes.'"

MOST UNFORGETTABLE ISLANDERS GAME

When the Islanders first came into existence, the franchise took part in an Expansion Draft, along with the Atlanta Flames, to procure talent from the existing NHL teams. And the very first player the Islanders selected was a player on the Boston Bruins by the name of Ed Westfall.

It certainly was a shock to the system for Westfall, who had essentially been groomed to be a Bruin ever since his teen years. Plus, he'd won two Stanley Cups during his 11-years in Boston. So why would he want to go to a place that he readily admitted he had never heard of -- Long Island.

But it turned out to be a blessing for Westfall as he joined a team that experienced numerous magical moments during his tenure. And it all started when then Isles G.M. Bill Torrey came to Westfall before the start of the Islanders' inaugural season (1972-73) and asked him to be the team captain. It was an honor for Westfall and one he gladly accepted. It was also a title he carried in a distinguished manner from Day One until the 1976-77 season.

And never was his leadership more important than during the Islanders' 1975 Quarter-Finals series against the Pittsburgh Penguins.

The Isles fell behind in the series 3-0 and were on the verge of being swept, when Head Coach Al Arbour gathered Westfall and his teammates at center ice for a chat.

WESTFALL: "Everybody knew what we had to do. And, of course, Al Arbour was a big part of that. I remember and it has been chronicled many times about, one day on the ice, I think when we were down three to Pittsburgh, he always crowded the players around at center ice so that nobody could hear it except the players. And he asked, 'is there anybody here who has any doubts that we can come back and win the next game and go on to win the series? And if you have any doubts, just go in and take your stuff and leave.'

"It was food for thought for everybody. And, of course, that was the mood. We'd come that far and no one ever expected us to make the playoffs, never mind get as far as we'd gotten. So, it really hit home. That was quite a moment there at center ice and food for thought and we all reflected on that."

Well, Westfall and his teammates certainly took Arbour's words to heart as they stormed back and won Games 4, 5 and 6 to force a winner-take-all Game 7 that would be played in Pittsburgh.

WESTFALL: "You can't change anything. It's an attitude. That's a big thing, to have a positive attitude. And in any of those games coming back you just have to remember it. And there's an old cliché and it still works, it's still part of hockey, 'when you're down, it comes to a shift at a time.'

"That was really echoed around the dressing room, time and time again. We were all talking to each other, yelling at each other, come on, we can do this. No one wants to be the weak link of a chain. So, everybody's got to do his best. Don't try to overdo your job. Just do what you're supposed to do. Play your game and we'll be okay. That was the kind of attitude that prevailed and that's really playoff hockey."

With the momentum on their side the Isles prepared for a Game 7 that could very well serve as a defining moment for the fledgling franchise. And it all started in the locker room before the game.

WESTFALL: "When we got to the dressing room, there was a little bit of a crescendo building, because we knew the importance (of the game). We had to win one more hockey game to get through this series.

It all starts with the first shift. Let's see if we can win a shift at a time. It just kind of builds itself.

"It also has to do with what the other team is thinking. They were probably thinking, 'Holy sh*t, we could end up losing four-straight games to the lowly Islanders. They're going to roll over us and we were the second-best team in the division.' So, I'm sure we had the momentum factor. You can't sit there in the dressing room before the game and say, 'we've got them because we've won three-straight.' We had great respect for the Pittsburgh Penguins at that time and they were a wonderful hockey team. So we were not going to take anything for granted. They were not going to let us beat them. We were going to have to beat them.

"The fact was the game was in their building and they had a lot of firepower on that team. And just the fact that in their building, we were tied with them (0-0) through two periods. Once that game got into the third period, you kind of had a feeling that whoever scored (first) was going to win the game, but you couldn't count on it. But you're always hoping that, because of the tightness of the game and I mean it was flying back-and-forth. You're caught up in the moment of trying not to let your teammates down, but you're still trying to think positively.

"Throughout that whole game, that's really the way we were. We were always encouraged, because we were such an underdog. We were encouraged by the fact that we were tied with them and it was the seventh game. We've got this much invested in it boys, so let's pour a little bit more on if we've got it. We've got to dig deeper because you know that they're going to. That really carried the whole game.

"(And, of course,) there wasn't a whole lot to cheer about at that point (for the fans). So, little things like that you can take as a positive. The fans hadn't really had too much to cheer about (at that point) because these stumble bums out of Long Island had done a lot of damage so far; not only to Pittsburgh, but to the other playoff teams in The League. All of a sudden we had gained some respect in the fan's eyes and also in the team you're playing against."

That respect may have been growing, but it wasn't yet secure. And then Westfall changed all that with 14:42 gone by in the third period.

WESTFALL: "You're just reacting to the moment. We were in the Pittsburgh end of the ice and Bert Marshall was back at the point. The puck got passed back to Bert Marshall and the circumstances worked out. I was down in the right corner, I was playing right-wing at the time and I started to move out towards the front of the net. And Bert spotted me, I guess, and threw me the puck. I took it on my forehand, but the only thing I could do was shoot it backhand.

"So I just took about one step and I fired it at the net. I wasn't picking a corner or picking this, I just let go with a backhand and Gary Inness had kind of dropped down on his knees in a butterfly thing or whatever they call it. And it went right over his shoulder into the net. It was that simple. And there was still five-minutes to go in the game, I believe. It was near the end of the game. We still had to go another five-minutes after that without letting them get one. Anyway, it was pretty exciting."

From there the Islanders made sure Westfall's goal stood as the series-winner, thus capping off a historic comeback and kick starting the celebration.

WESTFALL: "Traditionally, in hockey, you celebrate with your teammates. And particularly in our case, there was a gathering of players at our end of the ice. And you always hope that when you go to shake hands at the end of a series that you're the ones with the smiles.

"(Then, in the locker room) I remember I was beat emotionally and just tired physically. So I sat in the dressing room with all my stuff. And when I finally got my skates off, by the time I kind of finished reflecting, everybody had showered, changed and they were gone. I was there with the two trainers and they were looking at me.

"So, all of a sudden I look around and I'm alone. I finally got in the shower and changed. Then I walked out of the dressing room and Syl Apps, who was one of the wonderful, wonderful players from Pittsburgh, was walking by our dressing room.

"He said, 'Eddie, what are you, what's going on?' He said, 'where's your team?' I said, 'everybody's gone Syl. It took me a long time to get out of my uniform and get changed. Here I am.' And he said, 'where are you going?' I said, 'you know what Syl, I don't know. The guys have all left. They're all going to celebrate.' And he said, 'well, come out with us.' So I went with the Pittsburgh Penguins and I sat with the Pittsburgh Penguins half the night. I was with them until like two or three in the morning, when I (finally) went back to the hotel. So I ended up celebrating our victory with the team we just beat."

A PICTURE IS WORTH 1,000 WORDS

WESTFALL: "I won two Stanley Cups in Boston and nothing is greater than the first Stanley Cup when you win it. When you're on a team and you've dreamt about it your whole life, winning the Stanley Cup is paramount to any kid growing up the way most of us grew up. It has a tremendous significance.

"But I always thought that, that 1975 hockey team, that I was lucky enough to be a part of, was the second most wonderful thing I did. The fellows who played on that team, they had heart, let me tell you. We may not have been as good as a whole lot of other players and teams, but we certainly took that a long, long way with just the desire of the whole organization to succeed.

"So my moment, as an Islander, would be, in the big picture of that season and narrowed down to that playoff year, because the next series we almost did it back-to-back. I would say, that year, that particular series against Pittsburgh. And then as a selfish point, being lucky enough to be in the right spot at the right time to score the goal."

23 ALYSE ZWICK (ISLANDERS IN-ARENA HOST)
CAPTAIN TAVARES CLINCHES ISLES FIRST PLAYOFF SERIES
WIN SINCE 1993
(@BARCLAYS CENTER)
APRIL 24, 2016
NYI 2, FLA 1 (2OT)

BACKGROUND

Not all media members are created the same. Some know from an early age that they want to be reporters and then do everything they can to follow their dreams. Then there are others who sort of stumble into becoming members of the media later on.

Now, it doesn't really matter which path one takes to become a member of the media so long as once they do so they are good at what they are assigned to do. And it's especially helpful when you manage to connect -- in a positive way -- with the fan base of the team or teams you are assigned to cover.

Plus, there are many different ways one can be assigned to cover a team or teams; especially in hockey. There is the traditional beat writer, the columnist, the play-by-play -- TV or radio -- the color commentator -- TV or radio -- the in-studio host, the intermission host, the between the benches reporter, the pre- and post-game analyst and last but certainly not least, the in-arena host.

Each of these assignments is crucial to the overall presentation and coverage of an NHL game. But there is one who has to interact with the fans more so than the rest and that is the in-arena host, whose job can be a tiring one -- physically and mentally.

The in-ring host has to balance talking with players, coaches, officials and the fans, while also dealing with team promotions -- like toy giveaways -- and making sure that everyone in the arena is as engaged as possible.

And when the Islanders moved to Barclays Center in Brooklyn at the start of the 2015-16 season, they were searching for the right person to be their in-arena host. That person ended up being Alyse Zwick.

ZWICK: "I was in New York City news and wanted to be part of a team atmosphere as I was formerly with the NY Jets. (One day) my friend, a former Ice-Girl, told me about the audition, as she knew I was in broadcasting, loved the team and had worked in professional sports (previously). I auditioned after standing in a line with other candidates that wrapped around Barclays Center. (And eventually the Islanders picked me)."

Not only did Zwick get the gig, but she held onto it for four-years -- through the 2018-19 season -- and was absolutely beloved by Islanders fans, as well as by her constant companion, Team Mascot, Sparky The Dragon. With how beloved she was -- and still is -- let's take a minute to learn a little bit more about her backstory.

ZWICK: "In 2009, I earned the title of Miss New York 2009 for the Miss America Organization. And at the 2010 Miss America Pageant, I was the preliminary winner of the Lifestyle and Fitness Award, also known as the swimsuit competition.

"I've also done a lot of advocacy work in the war veteran's community, which I was inspired to do by my grandfather, a decorated WWII Army Veteran. In addition to my regular jobs, I am also the official spokesperson for the United War Veterans Council in New York City and host the annual New York City Veterans Day Parade LIVE from 5th avenue."

That's quite the impressive resume and for Alyse's efforts as an advocate, she has been recognized at the State and National levels. And according to her online biography, "in 2019 she was chosen by Starz Network and Steven Soderbergh to moderate their Tribeca Film Festival premiere of Leavenworth, a controversial true crime series shining light on and analyzing the military system at large."

All in all, Zwick is a jack-of-all-trades and has rightly been recognized by her peers and her fans for her hard work.

A GLIMPSE INTO THE LIFE OF AN NHL IN-ARENA HOST

ZWICK: "I had so many special days and games with the team. However, I think the first time I got to interview all of the legends in a panel style interview for season-ticket holders was just really special.

"The Isles Legends are such a special group of iconic athletes and the ability to interview them and get to know them over the years was pretty incredible and very special to me.

"(But as for the games themselves), before the game I would stand in the corner and run through all of my lines and talk to myself. My game ops crew eventually just got used to the routine of me talking to myself.

"I also always enjoyed coffee chats with some of our players before the games. It was nice to hear where their heads were at going into the games and going over trivia questions with some of the seasoned players. Working with the game operations officials and behind the scenes side of the game was always a lot of fun too. I loved the rapport everyone had with one another and the excitement each person had coming to work every day. After all, our jobs are unique and exciting and it was nice to be around people who loved what they did too.

"During each game, I was so busy running to each segment that there really wasn't an actual routine. And after the games, I was tired...in a good way. I loved every second of it, but there were moments when one second I would have to be at one-side of the arena and would run to the other to set up for live shots. I definitely got my steps in during games, so I definitely enjoyed decompressing on the subway with my headphones in and low-key music.

"(One game in particular that stands out to me was during) my first season, when Alan Quine assisted on John Tavares' game-winning goal in double-overtime if Game 6 against the Panthers to advance us to the second-round for the first time since 1993. I just happened to be right on the glass during that moment.

"(Overall) I loved, loved, loved, loved covering games. I loved seeing the fans, seeing their families grow up, hearing about the schools they were getting into, etc., all while enjoying a fun and fast game I grew up watching. It was a great family atmosphere and I was so blessed and grateful to be a part of it (for the seasons I was with the Islanders)."

A PICTURE IS WORTH 1,000 WORDS

ZWICK: ""(My favorite moment would be) singing carpool karaoke with Isles legend, Clark Gillies, which was pretty special. I was driving the Isles truck around Brooklyn and while we were singing he told me stories about his family and his skates being in the Hall of Fame.

It was just a very special moment and I loved how the fans received it too."

MESSAGES TO ISLANDERS FANS

NEIL BEST: "As a hockey guy, I always have a special place for hockey, hockey fans, hockey players and hockey writers. But the great thing about the Islanders and their fans, which I hope and expect to continue when they move to Belmont, is that they're this unique little niche in the New York sports world where all of the teams in the other three sports have these broad, region-wide fan bases that are not unique.

"I mean, I know there are Islanders fans outside of Long Island, but obviously most of them are on Long Island. So I just think Islanders fans should embrace the fact, not only that they're fans of this team, but also that it's a unique relationship with the fans because of the fact it's the one team that's directly associated with Long Island. And that doesn't mean you have to root for the Islanders over the Rangers.

"But I do think it is something that makes Islanders fans unique to all the teams in the area, that they've embraced this team, just like fans of the Yankees would. The difference is, that they have a more concentrated fandom because it's based in a smaller geographic area. And that's something unique about watching that team and rooting for that team. And I think that's one of the great things about this Belmont thing versus Brooklyn, is that, that will help continue that kind of vibe into the future, hopefully, for the next whatever, next 30-40 years, or however long that building's supposed to stand. And then for whatever arena comes next.

"So that is a cool thing about Islanders fans. We see it on our (Newsday's) website. There's no team in New York that drives as much traffic to our website as the Islanders, because, A) because we cover them so thoroughly. But B) there's this smaller group than Yankees fans, but it's the most passionate group of any of the teams that we cover as far as what we see on our website and in our print edition."

GREG BOURIS: "They (the fans) can't forget the roots of the franchise, the men behind that franchise and what they demonstrated. Not only the great players and what they accomplished by playing together as a team and the life lessons, I think they learned from the management of Bill Torrey and Al Arbour, in what they created. So, my message to Islanders fans, from any generation, is to understand the history of the team, understand that your team, your favorite team, played a very significant role in advancing not only the sport of hockey, in the expansion era, but also the sports industry, in terms of all of those other things I talked about.

"The cable TV aspect, as well as the management style that was set forth by Bill Torrey, by hiring good people and then getting out of their way and letting them do their jobs.
Being visionaries really allowed the team to flourish and build a history that is not matched by many organizations. So, despite the hardships that have transpired, maybe use that history and embrace that history to strive to see if there's a way to emulate or replicate it.

"It's impossible to think there'll be another stretch like that. But in terms of making the playoffs and being a dominant force to play against, regardless of your ability, I think is the takeaway there. And I think they're doing that now. They are not a lot of superstars on the team right now, but they are playing 'THAT' way. That was always the mantra in the locker room. It's the name on the front of the sweater and not the name on the back that means the most. And that's how they're playing today. That's something they always have to do to embrace the history and to use history as motivation for the future."

LARRY BROOKS: "I mean, it's just such a great heritage. Such a great, great heritage that it's unfortunate that it's been such a long time for the people there. They have good people there. A good foundation there. It is a history that should be celebrated."

FRANK BROWN: "I covered the Philadelphia Flyers' Stanley Cup wins in the mid-70s. I covered the Montreal Canadiens Stanley Cup wins at the end of the '70s. I covered all of the Islanders' Stanley Cups in the early '80s and all of the Edmonton Stanley Cups that followed. Throw in The Miracle at Lake Placid and I've covered a ton of champions. I would place ahead of all others the Islanders' talent, their character, their courage, their resilience, their versatility, their determination and their standards of excellence.

"They won 19 consecutive playoff series. Bill Torrey built a team that could win any way it needed to. Whether it took a skating game or a checking game, whether it took fighting or finesse, whether it was a tight game or a blowout, the Islanders I covered always found a way to win. I don't know what higher compliment can be paid. Islanders fans were blessed with more than a dynasty; they were witnesses to an era of hockey majesty the likes of which will never reappear."

BRENDAN BURKE: "I mean, really the one thing I would say to every Islanders fan is, thank you for accepting me. I was coming in following Howie (Rose) and following that lineage, including Jiggs (McDonald) and I was a 32-year-old AHL radio broadcaster who no one had ever heard of. I would've been very easy to not like and this fan base, from day one, gave me an opportunity to win them over.

"I have to thank them for that because I'm not sure every broadcaster, in every other market, for any other team, was given that opportunity sometimes. I have become an Islander through and through and they've allowed me to do that. So thank you to all the Islanders fans for giving me a chance to be the new voice of the team or to be THE voice of the team. It's a special feeling."

PAT CALABRIA: "Those Islander teams from '80 to '83 and even '84, when they lost in the Final, those were some of the greatest teams in the history of the National Hockey League. There's simply no disputing that. If you watch those games on video and I used to watch cassettes of those games, that team's speed, defense, goaltending, you wanted to fight them, they'd fight you. You wanted to try to bully them; it wasn't going to happen anymore. And I remember going into the Edmonton series in '83, which was when they swept the Oilers and they went in as underdogs.

"The defending three-time champions going into a series as underdogs. I don't know if that had ever happened. And I remember a writer in Edmonton saying, 'the Islanders are not even going to be able to compete in the series. They had never seen an offense like the Oilers have.' And I said, 'it may be true, but I don't think the Oilers have ever seen fore-checking like they were going to see in this series.' And of course the Islanders fore-checked the heck out of them. And one of the great unanticipated events in that series was that Ken Morrow outscored the great Wayne Gretzky."

HAWLEY CHESTER: "I loved that period, that first growth of a team that was 12-60-6 its first year. We were referred to as the 'Hapless' Islanders by every media member in the sports world. We were the 'Hapless' Islanders and Bill Torrey and I rejected that; routinely. Everywhere we went people wanted us to be the laughable Mets, a joke, a goofy, funny team and we rejected that everywhere we went. I did TV and radio and I routinely barked back at anybody when they used the word hapless to my face because we had a plan and I was part of that original plan.

"From day one there was a plan and the late-Bill Torrey would tell you the same thing. From the first time he shook hands with Roy (Boe) as the GM, to the time he ended his career on Long Island, there was a plan in place. There was always a plan and part of the plan was we were new. We were never going to be as good as the Flames, if you will, because we started on the same day. They were going to be in the Western Division. We weren't. We were in the Eastern Division. We were going to be at the bottom of Eastern Division because if you look, all of the Original Six teams were in our division, plus, some of the better expansion teams.

"We had no chance of surviving or thriving as an expansion team. We had to basically start from scratch and build each block. The way we were, we wanted to not worry about what our record was going to be in the beginning because we knew we were going to be lousy. We knew we were going to suffer. But we also knew that there was a future out there in the amateur ranks. There were players like Denis Potvin and Bryan Trottier who we knew were coming. And if we did our job, we would be getting those players and that we'd be building our team, literally, with those kinds of draft choices and that the people who were there at the beginning, were probably not going to be with us for very long.

"We didn't care about picking the best players in the Expansion Draft. We knew that those players were not our future. Those players were going to be in the past. But we had to start somewhere. So we started and we suffered. We were the worst team in the history of the NHL at that time. Fortunately, we were beaten out by the Washington Capitals shortly thereafter, but at the time nobody had ever had a record like ours. Being the 'Hapless' Islanders; we rejected that everywhere we went. But it was a tag that was put on us by the media and they tried to perpetuate that everywhere we went.

"Well, we didn't believe in that. We knew we had a plan and we knew what the plan was and it was going to work if we stuck to it. And we did. We stuck to the plan. We suffered a little bit because financially it hurt everything else. We knew it was going to hurt. But we also knew the Rangers were going to be the best team in town.

"We were going to be compared to the Rangers, who were going to be in our division. No matter what we were going to have to play them, four, five, six, eight times; however much it was. We knew that most of the fans would be Rangers fans. But what I can say is that

Islanders fans grew out of being former-Rangers fans and became loyal Islanders fans and grew with us. And for that, I am eternally grateful."

BRIAN COMPTON: "Just being there and knowing everything that they've (the fans) gone through. I say this a lot, don't ever, ever let anyone tell you that nobody cares about that hockey team (the Islanders) because that's simply not the truth. I think even now, even in the past two years, despite all the changes they've made with Lou (Lamoriello) and Barry (Trotz), sweeping the Penguins last year and (collecting) 103-points, having home-ice for the first time since 1988, all the good things they've done, it just seems like there's still a lack of respect across the board.

"Maybe not from opposing players, but there's still a lot of disbelief I think in the team and what they're doing. I think that's just part of it. It just seems like no matter what they do, it's not good enough for people outside this market. And maybe even for some people inside this market too. Whether it's The Daily News or The Post, still not being there on a daily basis to cover the team, even though they play in this market just like everybody else.

"There's still this belief that nobody cares about them. I just think it's completely ridiculous and we've seen it when the team is good. The fans will show up and that's really all they've ever wanted. They wanted a product to believe in and support. And they have it now with the new building on the horizon, the infrastructure they have in place and the ownership that is in place providing the resources they need to be good year in and year out. There's no reason to think that they're not going to be good for a really long time. And that's really great news for all those people."

ERIC COMPTON: "Cherish the sport. Admire the players for what they could do because it is the most specialized talent in all of sports. And I think that's why it's the one the fewest people actually play, because it is so difficult to play. To be able to skate, do what they do and do it at the speed they do it and be able to hit and take shots and stop shots and be absolutely fearless and know you're going to get hit in the corners and to be able to do what they do; just do what I do, admire the sport for what it is and admire the players for how difficult it is to do what they do.

"I mean, anyone else in the world could go out tomorrow and pick up a basketball and might be able to shoot a basketball. Anybody else could go out and swing a bat and maybe be able to hit a baseball or softball a little bit. Anybody can hit a golf ball, maybe not well, but they could do it. Anybody can kick a soccer ball. How many people can go out and play hockey at a high level? It is the most difficult sport to play.

It's the greatest sport to watch live. And I would say that to Islanders fans everyday. Cherish what you're watching.

"This is the greatest indoor sport to watch live. There is nothing, nothing that compares to the Stanley Cup playoffs. You get a one-goal game in the Stanley Cup playoffs; especially late in the series, there is nothing like the pressure in that. There is nothing like the drama that you get from a Stanley Cup playoff game. Again, I've watched everything. I go back and I've seen the Mets win twice and I've seen the Giants win four-times in football and I've seen the Knicks win twice in basketball. Nothing is like hockey. It is the greatest sport.

"I know it's tough to watch on TV because it's tough to follow the puck sometimes. And I know people talk about, 'well it's only the fourth sport because people don't watch it.' The NHL is very happy with their ratings because they have their core. It's a religion. Hockey is a religion. And once you get it, you don't let go of it. And it's going to be like that. I mean, once it gets in your blood, it stays there and hopefully you have enough good moments that just keep you coming back.

"There's always that hope that your team can turn things around. Hockey is just the greatest sport to watch live and you should just watch it and enjoy it. And yes, you're not going to win every year, but you know what, there's always next year."

STAN FISCHLER: "My message to Islanders fans is that the fans made my career as much as any person, factors or anything else, because they provided me with a lot of motivation, a lot of energy. And when all is said and done, I was more fan than journalist. I always rooted hard. When I did Rangers games, I rooted for the Rangers. Why? Because I wanted to do a happy dressing post-game; I always wanted to do a happy dressing. And, Islanders fans are a special breed, they suffered at the beginning and they suffered right up until they made that playoffs (1975) and I started broadcasting. The Rangers killed them in Game 2 at The Coliseum. It was very iffy.

"It was nice to be with a brand new team, to see it grow and to see the fans develop. I have said it many times that, I've lived to be 87, because of hockey and other factors like family. But hockey has kept the juices going. It could be being on Twitter tweeting. It could be watching a game. It could be doing anything and I bonded with Islanders fans. It didn't happen right away. It took a while. But then I did the four dynasty years. We suffered badly in '78 when the Leafs beat us. We suffered worse in '79 when the Rangers beat us. But you know what they say, 'pain and progress are inseparable.'"

ALAN HAHN: "The message I would have for them (the fans) is that they are the sole reason why this franchise still exists. And I don't know if you can say that about a lot of franchises, because in any other city or even any other type of team, this franchise would have either folded or moved by now. After everything it's been through, but you can still feel the passion of the fan base. It's legitimate, even though it's not as large as it used to be. And you have the Rangers, who obviously dominate when it comes to popularity for hockey.

"But there was always something special about the passion, the loyalty, the determination, everything about this fan base would tell the owners who came after, whether it was Charles Wang and then after him, Scott Malkin and Jon Ledecky. Now, it was evident, this is not a team, it's not a franchise you give up on. And give credit to Gary Bettman, who grew up on Long Island, who always knew that. They've (The NHL) moved franchises.

"The Atlanta Thrashers were failing. They went to Winnipeg. There were places where you just said, 'this is not working.' I mean, they moved Quebec out of Quebec. He would never let the Islanders move. And it was because of the fan base and because of how passionate and loyal they were. They knew that if they just got it right, it would thrive and it was all because of them (the fans).

"So I always tell fans that when they say, 'Oh, you know what this franchise has been through,' and it's amazing. They talk about the owners who saved the franchise and I said, 'no, no, no, no, the fans saved this franchise.' Their loyalty is what saved the franchise, because in any other place, this franchise would have folded or moved by now."

SHANNON HOGAN: "Be true to yourself. I think part of what this franchise does well is the fans are authentic and I think that the players know that. And I think they realize that's part of the identity of this team and the franchise. So, I guess I would say, 'keep wearing the jerseys that make you happy, wearing the crazy hair, the cowboy hats, painting your face and bringing your kids, because it's a family and it's got to continue from generation to generation.'

"Those stories, those memories are passed down and that's the stuff that the players thrive on, the history of this team, but also the next generation is looking at the past stories their parents have told them, the grandparents had told them and also excited about the future of the team, whatever the direction is. So I think I would just say, 'be true to yourself and how you are as a fan and what brings you joy, because ultimately the players feed off of that.'"

CHRIS KING: "I would just like to thank the entire fan base of the NY Islanders for being as passionate about this team as I am. Whenever I meet fans, they always tell me how my calls resonate with them because of the emotion and intensity that I will always have for this club, having literally grown up with the team since it arrived on Long Island back in 1972, when I was only 11 years old and finally had an NHL team to call my own."

ALLAN KREDA: "Well, this is a franchise that went to five-straight Stanley Cups in the '80s, so for any watcher, fan, or person who was interested in hockey in those years, whether you rooted for the Islanders or the Rangers, or hockey in general, you had to admire what that meant. It's never been done since. The chances are nearly astronomical it'll ever happen again. I think the franchise's genetics; the franchise's DNA is in those wins and is in what came out of those wins.

"There's always that kernel of possibility because they did it before, so maybe they can do it again. So, as I would say to Rangers fans, Devils fans or to any team's fans whose won a Stanley Cup within the last decade or two or three, there's always hope. But for the Islanders, because of their history, because of guys like (Bobby) Nystrom, (Clark) Gillies, Butch Goring and John Tonelli, who are around the team, there's something that's got to rub off eventually and set them on that course again.

"How could they not, even though it's now been 35-years since they were in The Final and it is 40-years coming up they won the first Cup on Nystrom's goal. It's part of the history in a way that that lives on everyday. And the fact they've been back at The Coliseum in this weird split recently, it has brought it back even more so. Never give up hope."

STEVE MEARS: "The message would probably be to keep the passion. There are very few fan bases like the Islanders fan base. We travel; we go to all the buildings. I've worked for a couple of teams now and it's just very unique. There are fervent fan bases. We know there are great fan bases in Canada and we've got a great one here in Pittsburgh. You've got multiple teams in the New York area. You've got other cities like Chicago and Boston and the Original Six.

"But there's something unique about the Islander fans, the Long Island community, the history of the team with the greatness and then the struggle, which has happened. And now it's great to see the team coming back to prominence here. So, they've been through a lot and through all of it that core fan base has been so passionate.

"So I would just say, moving forward, keep that passion, no matter where the team goes, up or down. We've seen the highest of highs with the Islanders dynasty and the lowest of lows with the years of struggle and mismanagement. There aren't many franchises who can say they've had that gamut of emotions from their fan experience.

"There are very few teams, probably in sports, who can say they've had that type of polar opposites. So, whatever it may be, whatever the future holds, I would say just keep the passion because there's nothing quite like the Islanders fan base. It's incomparable just because of the course of history the team has gone through."

BARRY MEISEL: "This was a team that had such a great tradition and such a work ethic. Bill Torrey, the General Manager and Al Arbour, the coach, were two Hall of Famers, two of the most successful and towering figures in hockey history. That team set an example for many teams in the NHL. And I think Islanders fans appreciated and knew that back then. So my message to Islanders fans now is, you had one of the most impressive, formidable, successful franchises in hockey history in that 1980's New York Islanders group."

BOBBY NYSTROM: "I would just say thank you. Thank you for welcoming us and taking us into your arms. You are just the greatest fans ever. It was a community that we really came to love and many of us stayed there because it was so enjoyable. The people really took us in and then we really tried to live and assist in some of the ventures they were doing. The charities and things like that. But more than anything else, I would just say thank you for welcoming us in and for being the best fans ever."

GLENN "CHICO" RESCH: "When I think of Islanders fans, it always puts a smile on my face. Really nothing in Long Island ever happened that wasn't a team-fan combination, relationship. I mean the Islanders fans were great. We had Islander dinner where fans would come out to the rink. They were also enthusiastic. Mostly, for all of us young guys, coming to New York and most not being from New York, to feel the experience of what the Islander fans created, with the energy, with the love of the team and the love of the players. Of course we had success, which helped.

"I remember everybody had a fan club. You don't see that anymore. You walked out of the rink at the end of the game and the fans were there and you'd talk to them and shake hands or whatever. It was a different world then. But I think, for all of us, the fans gave us confidence. When you're a player, you're obviously playing because of the paycheck you get. But you're also playing because you want to have personal success.

"However, there comes a point and it did in Long Island, where you really want to please the fans. You just saw the joy in them when we were doing well. We were in the shadow of the Rangers and they just felt like, 'Hey, this Islanders team can take on the Rangers.' And so, we felt, not only their enjoyment but also their enthusiasm and the confidence building in them that then also built in us. Whenever I think of my days on Long Island, it was really me connecting with the fans and the fans connecting with us players. I've talked to many, many Islanders fans since then and they talk about those years in glowing reports. They said it was the best years on Long Island. And I have to agree."

HOWIE ROSE: "Thanks for accepting me. You're all in my heart. I am thrilled, almost beyond my ability to describe, the news that the Belmont arena is going to be a reality, because if any franchise in pro sports has deserved their very own state-of-the-art building for as many years as they've waited, it's definitely the Islanders fans. And I am just excited as can be about the fact the Islanders are going to have that new building and that this team is where it belongs, on Long Island to stay."

NEIL SMITH: "I think that the message would be just that I was really thrilled to be a part of the Islanders and to be able to be lucky enough to be there at that particular time. I think they're going in the right direction right now. They've got a great General Manager (Lou Lamoriello). They've got a great coach (Barry Trotz). They seem to have a real stable organization now. And I think it's a matter of time before they are able to be back up in the group of teams who are contenders for the Stanley Cup.

"I don't know if they'll ever be a dynasty again, but I do think they're back. They can be back as a true Stanley Cup contender in the not too distant future. But, reflecting back on my days in the early-80's, I'm so thankful I got that opportunity and that I was there and that I was smart enough to know that money doesn't mean anything when you're that young. If you get an opportunity, take the opportunity. Don't worry about money. That's what I would say. I loved my time there so much."

ARTHUR STAPLE: "I admire their (the fans) passion and commitment to a team that hasn't always shown them the same love and respect in return over the decades. I can't count how many Islanders fans I've met, who are not new fans, who are in their 30's or 20's and who had never seen a really good team because they missed the dynasty era by a little too much. And yet, they still show up every night here and sometimes show up on the road and make the Islanders a big part of their lives.

"I got into this profession because I loved sports, but not because I loved a specific team and I'm always in admiration of people who can have that much passion and excitement for one team to try to see them do well. It's always fueled their interactions with me and it fuels what I do. It's a special relationship and I appreciate it a lot."

JOHN STERLING: "I love the Islanders fans. When I was doing the games, the Islanders were just becoming the team that would eventually win four-straight Cups in the early-80s. They hadn't gotten there yet, but they were improving every year. Bill Torrey and company,

Jimmy Devellano, was the big scout and look who they drafted, my goodness, (Denis) Potvin and (Bryan) Trottier and (Clark) Gillies and (Bobby) Nystrom and the big one, getting Mike Bossy. They built this tremendous team and they would win at home.

"I had a partner on the air who really became like a brother to me. We were really close. He's passed on unfortunately. His name was Bob Lawrence. And he was great. It was so great for me to broadcast these games with a guy I absolutely loved. Great voice. Great style. It was such an unusual time in my life. I was doing Morgan State football. So, in November and December, they'd have an afternoon game somewhere in the South and I'd have to fly back and I'd get my car from Kennedy (Airport), get on the Belt Parkway and I'd end up just getting there (to The Coliseum). I mean it probably took years off my life.

"I'd get there, but Bob had everything in control and I'd sit down and he would say, 'and now with the play-by-play...' So that's what a great partner I had. For the Islanders fans, they sold the building out. We won almost all the time. Everyone shouted my 'Islander Goal! ISLANDER GOAL!' Bill Torrey used to do that too to me.

"Most guys say, 'he shoots, he scores!' But I didn't, I wanted to be ahead. I would say 'Goal! Islander Goal,' and then repeat. It was absolutely the true definition of it's a labor of love. It was my labor and I loved it."

RICH TORREY: "It's sort of changed now based on what I have just gone through in the last-year-and-a-half. But what they (the fans) meant (to me), the texts and things I've gotten in the last-year-and-a-half from Islanders fans, people who I have no idea who they are and how nice the messages were about my dad and about what those years meant to them.

"It meant the same to him. They meant the same to him. But those Islander fans, through the losing years and then through those Cup years and then even after when they struggled as he was trying to right the ship again and retool, they were so kind to him.

"He (my dad) loved them. He really did. I go back to the passion of the Islanders-Rangers rivalry and the passion the Islander fans had and the Ranger fans had for their teams. The way they treated him was so kind and he loved it. It surprised him. Or it never got old, let's put it that way. He never took it for granted."

ED WESTFALL: "Well, much like the teams they supported, they never gave up. Look at them now. I'm a big fan of the fans and I became one too. But the way they have conducted themselves through all of the bull that's gone on over the years with all the different owners. And I mean, there were just some terrible people who should never have even dreamed about owning a hockey team. The fans, the core of the fans, they stuck in there and they're still there. You go to an event today and I get lucky enough to do some of them and they are there.

"This new owner Jon Ledecky and his ownership team, these people are behind them, supporting them and they're getting it back because these new owners are supporting the fans. They're not taking them for granted like some of the others did.

"They truly work with the fans and support the fans. And so, people like myself and some of the other alumni, who really just drifted away. We weren't really welcomed into the Islander end of it anymore. We were kind of let go and that's okay. That's not poor us. But we always enjoyed the fact that we were past Islanders.

"Well, these fans and the love affair for the Islanders, with the ownership picking up on that and then just absolutely going overboard to bring the alumni back as part of the team and let the fans and alumni have wonderful moments together. And that's what they've done.

"Consequently, they've also hired some wonderful people to run the team. So, it's really building again. They're building some momentum. The fans are the number one thing. They are number one. And I admire them for standing with the team even though they've been kicked around a little bit. But they have. They have stuck in there and there's nothing but uphill from here."

ALYSE ZWICK: ""My time with the Islanders was so special to me. It was 4-years of my life that flew by and I cherished every moment. I became a die-hard fan that now bleeds blue and orange. I am genuinely grateful for each and every moment with every fan, player, official, security officer and anyone involved with the team. I will always remember how the team helped me learn how to be live every night and that gave me the confidence to know my talents were appreciated and loved. There is nothing like the Isles fan base. They are truly the best fans in The League and I couldn't be happier looking back on my time with The New York Islanders. They'll always hold a very special place in my heart."

ACKNOWLEDGEMENTS

For those who think that writing a book is easy, it's not. And you need more than just yourself to finish such a project. Therefore, it's important to thank those who have helped you along the way. So, I would like to acknowledge the following people for their roles in this project.

Neil Best, Greg Bouris, Larry Brooks, Frank Brown, Brendan Burke, Pat Calabria, Hawley Chester III, Brian Compton, Eric Compton, Stan Fischler, Alan Hahn, Shannon Hogan, Chris King, Allan Kreda, Steve Mears, Barry Meisel, Bobby Nystrom, Glenn "Chico" Resch, Howie Rose, Neil Smith, Arthur Staple, John Sterling, Rich Torrey, Ed Westfall and Alyse Zwick all took time out of their busy schedules to be interviewed for chapters in this book and told their stories with the same enthusiasm they share with the fans while doing their jobs.

Dan Schoenberg helped provide access to the subjects of this book.

My parents -- Mandi and Seth -- sister -- Tara -- grandparents -- Morton, Stanley, Yvonne and Zella -- uncles -- Andrew, Lenny, Scott and Glenn -- and aunts -- Yvonne, Anita and Brooke -- all of whom provided support throughout the book writing process.

My friends -- Samantha Bruno, Deanna Chillemi, Brittany Ciraolo, Taylor Chiaia, Lauren DeCordova, Jessica DiMari, Leanna Gryak, Stef Hicks, Maria Koutros, Christina Luddeni, Arianna Rappy, Michele Rosati, Amanda Sorrentino, Jessica Sorrentino, Brianna Torkel, Victoria Wehr, Maggie Wince, Jared Bell, Trevor Blenman, Andrew

Bodnar, Skylar Bonné, Walt Bonné, Danny Randell, Bobby Denver, Robert DeVita, Brandon Dittmar, Jared Fertig, Landon Goldfarb, Daniel Greene, Peter Koutros, Michael Manna, Matt Mattone, Logan Miller, Mike O'Brien, Dan O'Shea, Reid Packer, Chris Pellegrino, Max Rappy, Jason Russo, Aaron Shepard, Anthony Spadaro, William Storz and Joey Wilner -- all of whom provided assistance and support throughout the book process as well.

In addition, I would like to give a special shoutout to my friends, Peter Koutros and Mike O'Brien, both of whom implored me to do a book on the Islanders from the first time I said I was going to be an author.

And to my fellow media members/colleagues/etc. who have helped to guide and influence my career -- Kenny Albert, Pete Albietz, Michael Ali, Jeff Beukeboom, Justin Birnbaum, Martin Biron, Josh Bogorad, Amanda Borges, Ryan Braithwaite, Matt Calamia, Steve Cangialosi, Rick Carpiniello, Scott Charles, Ryan Chiu, Hayley Cohen, Russ Cohen, Charlie Cucchiara, Jack Curry, Ken Daneyko, John Davidson, Jeff Day, John Dellapina, Bob de Poto, Rachel Schwartz Dixon, Roland Dratch, Ron Duguay, Chris Ebert, Mike "Doc" Emrick, Katie Epifane McCarthy, Annie Fariello, John Fayolle, Jeff Filippi, Matt Fineman, Jim Fox, Jim Gallagher, John Giannone, Rod Gilbert, Butch Goring, Adam Graves, Andrew Gross, Larry Hirsch, Nick Holmer, Eric Hornick, Howie Karpin, Kelly Keogh, Rachel Krawsek, Don La Greca, Jon Lane, Paul Lauten, Jon Ledecky, Matt Loughlin, Dave Maloney, Mike Mancuso, Joel Mandelbaum, Dan Marrazza, Corey Masisak, Jim Matheson, Matt McConnell, Patrick McCormack, Kevin Meininger, Bob Melnick, Sal Messina, Joe Micheletti, Bobby Mills, Mike Morreale, Lucky Ngamwajasat, Michael Obernauer, Arda Ocal, Pat O'Keefe, Glenn Petraitis, Deb Placey, Brad Polk, Mike Richter, Dan Rosen, Sam Rosen, Mark Rosenman, Larry Roth, Chris Ryan, Bryce Salvador, Samuel Sandler, Leo Scaglione Jr., Sarah Servetnick, Ashley Scharge, Derek Stepan, Colin Stephenson, Jim Sullivan, Robert Taub, Al Trautwig, Leslie Treff, Steve Valiquette, Colleen Wagoner, Mollie Walker, Ryan Watson, Kevin Weekes, Craig Wolff, Cory Wright and Steve Zipay.

SOURCES

***NOTE:** All interviews were conducted either in-person, over the phone or via email in order to obtain the necessary quotes and information.*
***NOTE:** All statistics, dates, locations, etc. were gathered via box scores from NHL.com or Hockey-Reference.com.*

ABOUT THE AUTHOR

Matthew Blittner, born and raised in Brooklyn, New York, has been covering the New York Islanders, New Jersey Devils and New York Rangers for multiple publications since the beginning of the 2016-17 NHL season. Along the way, he has covered each of the teams' respective playoff runs over the past several seasons.

Among the publications Matthew Blittner has written for are: MSGNetworks.com, The Fischler Report, The Hockey News Magazine and NY Sports Day.

In addition to his responsibilities covering the NY/NJ hockey scene, Matthew obtained his Master's Degree in Sports Management from CUNY Brooklyn College in February of 2017 -- graduating with Summa Cum Laude honors.

Matthew's latest book, Unforgettable Islanders, is the third in his "Unforgettable Series Trilogy" and details the most significant games and moments in the careers of the broadcasters, writers, scouts, PR Directors and former players who have been around the team for generations.

Visit him on Twitter @MatthewBlittner.

www.ingramcontent.com/pod-product-compliance
Lightning Source LLC
LaVergne TN
LVHW051055080426
835508LV00019B/1892